THE CUSTOMER CENTRICITY PLAYBOOK

PETER FADER AND SARAH TOMS

THE CUSTOMER CENTRICITY PLAYBOOK

IMPLEMENT A WINNING STRATEGY DRIVEN BY CUSTOMER LIFETIME VALUE

Wharton
DIGITAL PRESS
Philadelphia

Published by Wharton Digital Press
The Wharton School
University of Pennsylvania
3620 Locust Walk
2000 Steinberg Hall-Dietrich Hall
Philadelphia, PA 19104
Email: whartondigitalpress@wharton.upenn.edu
Website: http://wdp.wharton.upenn.edu/

Ebook ISBN: 978-1-61363-091-4
Paperback ISBN: 978-1-61363-090-7

Contents

Preface

With 18 Olympic gold medals, Michael Phelps is the most decorated athlete of all time. It isn't surprising to learn that his training regimen would challenge demigods. At peak season, he clocks 50 miles per week in the pool and yet more hours in the gym. For other athletes wishing to join Phelps's ranks, this all sounds like a simple enough formula to replicate: train hard, eat smart, get stronger, perform better, win Olympic gold. The problem is that training and nutrition alone can't guarantee Phelps's impressive collection of Olympic bling.

Why not? If you train hard enough, you can achieve anything, right? In short, no. As a physical specimen, Michael Phelps was born to swim. His double-jointed ankles and size 14 feet work in conjunction with a double-jointed rib cage, meaning that his kick starts in his chest, generating a tremendous dolphin-like thrust. And even though Phelps is 6' 4", his arms measure 6' 7" from fingertip to fingertip, extending from a large and powerful torso that would be proportional for a man several inches taller than he stands. To add insult to injury for the mortals in the adjacent lanes wishing to challenge Phelps to a race, he produces less than half the lactic acid of other athletes, meaning he can quickly recover from physical exertion. Biomechanically and metabolically, Phelps was born with a substantial and natural advantage in the pool.

So what does Michael Phelps have to do with customer centricity? Well, his inherent *goodness* as a swimmer is an analog for one of the pillars of a customer-centric marketing strategy: Even before a customer makes their first purchase with you, much of their potential value is already there, just as Phelps's natural physical advantages were there when he was born. Sure, you can drag customers into the marketing and sales gym to develop their value a bit further, but by how much really depends on a number of predetermined factors that you don't have much, if any, control over. You certainly won't be able to transform the vast majority of your base into your best, most Phelps-like class of customer. On the other hand, knowing who your best customers are is not as clear as separating the winners from the losers in a quick swimming race. To get the clearest picture of a customer's value means harnessing the insights that come from playing a long game—one that projects their entire lifetime with you. That's what this book is about.

Introduction

We begin with a company that has been around for about 36 years, predating any modern notion of customer data analytics.[1] Back in 2013, it was loathed so intensely by its customers that it was named the worst company in America—for the second year in a row.[2] From the outside, this company appeared to be in such serious trouble that its days were surely numbered. Yet, over the past six years, its stock value has rebounded 1,000%,[3] and in 2017 it managed to clear a billion dollars in profit.[4] Would it surprise you to learn that the company in question is global gaming giant Electronic Arts (EA)?[5]

Sparking EA's miraculous turnaround was the company's realization that even if customers *look* the same on the surface, not all customers *are* the same—a principle that is fundamental to customer centricity. Today, we count EA in an elite class of companies that turned themselves around thanks to their steadfast commitment to their customer-centric strategy. We say *steadfast* because the turnaround has taken more than a decade to gain outward visible momentum, as reflected on Wall Street.

EA's turnaround actually began five long years before its stock price started to climb again, when a few data nerds working on the sales planning team decided to follow a hunch. They believed that the company was wasting vast resources in the way it invested its marketing budget—22% of revenue was spent on marketing at the time. Following this thread, the analysts wanted to see if they could use data to find a better way to advertise EA's games. Back then, much of the budget was spent right before a game launch and went to TV ads and other broadcast *spray-and-pray* approaches, but no one at EA had any clear goals in mind for how to measure the returns on this spending.

Figure I.1. EA NASDAQ Stock Prices, January 2012–July 2018

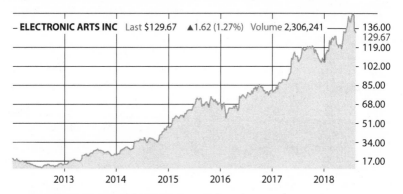

Source: "Electronic Arts Inc. (EA) Interactive Chart," Nasdaq, July 16, 2018, www.nasdaq.com/symbol/ea
/interactive-chart.

By optimizing a marketing mix algorithm, the data team was able to provide indisputable evidence to the decision makers at EA that the company was, indeed, spending its marketing dollars inefficiently. And thankfully for EA, the decision makers paid close attention when presented with alternatives. The result was a universal decrease in marketing dollars spent, with no negative impact to efficacy. This provided the first proof to EA that by leveraging data insights, it could forge a path to more successful decision making.

When EA purchased Playfish, a digital-first gaming company, in 2009, one of those data nerds from the sales planning team—Zachery Anderson—was appointed to lead the analytics and insights arm of EA Digital. This team made it their mission to mine whatever data they could find. By standardizing metrics, they created a unified, reliable way for the company to analyze hundreds of data points. The company was abuzz with the possibilities that these newfound insights heralded, but many EA employees also worried about the company's identity in light of this new flood of information. As Benjamin Tisdale, senior director of business analytics, reflected, many employees were asking, "Is data going to decide everything for us now? We're a creative company, and we didn't want to lose sight of who we are."[6]

Then, in 2013, Andrew Wilson was named EA's new CEO. Wilson decided to address head-on the tension between data-driven decision making and the need to protect the creativity of the game studios. By leveraging some key correlations that the Digital team's analysis revealed around engagement and customer value, Wilson championed a "Player First" mantra that translated into marching orders for the entire company to understand what exactly leads to higher player engagement.

As part of Wilson's "Player First" initiative, Anderson was asked to head up a new group called Global Analytics & Insights, which started to consolidate the company's understanding about players, showing that in-game engagement was a good proxy for the future value of individual players. In fact, engagement was the single best predictor for whether a customer would purchase other games in the future. This finding may seem obvious now, but for a company that was not digitally native and had spent most of its history thinking about its customers monolithically, this pivotal insight ignited a transformation that has touched every aspect of how the company thinks about its customers and how it designs games tailored to attract and retain its best customers.

EA's culture has since matured to a point where it values data and creativity equally, recognizing that these two approaches are symbiotic. The game designers embrace the insights data provide about player engagement, which helps inform what specifically is working and what needs to improve in the games they're producing. The studios aren't necessarily living and breathing in data in the same way the data teams are, but they are using these insights as guideposts to help scaffold ideas as they brainstorm new game ideas.

Certainly, the financial health of the company tells us this approach is working—really well! But if player engagement is one of the best indicators of the future value of EA's customers, then the recent stats about the popularity of EA's games are the best news of all. EA's 2017 end-of-year fiscal report stated: "EA was the #1 publisher on PlayStation®4 and Xbox One consoles in the Western World for fiscal 2017, based on available sources and EA estimates."[7]

EA is an almost-perfect case study in implementing a successful customer-centric business strategy. EA shows us how a firm can maximize its long-term financial value—and set itself up for long-term success—by drawing on the current and future needs of customers to guide the development and delivery of a company's products. Granted, the route to becoming a customer-centric company is not always simple or direct; in fact, some companies that think they're already customer centric don't even have a clear understanding of what customer centricity actually *is*, much less how it should be executed effectively.

Thankfully, that's where *The Customer Centricity Playbook* comes in.

About This Book

The Customer Centricity Playbook will guide you through the specifics of many customer centricity success stories, providing you with a 360-degree analysis of all the elements that support customer centricity in an organization. You will learn to

- develop a customer-centric strategy for your organization;
- understand the right way to think about customer lifetime value (CLV);
- make informed investments in sales, marketing, and customer service based on the customer life cycle;
- foster a culture that sustains customer centricity;
- understand the link between customer lifetime value and market valuation; and
- understand customer relationship management (CRM) systems, as they are a vital underpinning for all these areas through the valuable insights they provide

We lay out a straightforward methodology and set of concepts that are essential considerations for any organization looking to become customer centric. In fact, the goal of wanting to better explain the underlying principles of customer centricity is what brought us, your authors, together as collaborators.

Why We Wrote This Book

When we met in 2013, Peter's first book, *Customer Centricity: Focus on the Right Customers for Strategic Advantage*, had recently been published. It was one of the first on the subject intended for a general business audience, and it had also been translated into Chinese, Korean, and Portuguese, revealing global interest in the topic.

Peter was on the hunt for a capstone experience for students of his customer centricity MBA course at The Wharton School that would bring all the concepts of the course together in a challenging and realistic way. Sarah had recently become the director of Wharton's Al West Jr. Learning Lab, a collaborative incubator for driving the development of groundbreaking, award-winning, high-tech applications in education. When Sarah heard about Peter's desire to create an immersive learning experience for his students, she jumped at the chance to collaborate with him. She started by reading *Customer Centricity*.

Together, we created Wharton's Customer Centricity Simulation, a game that realistically simulates the acquisition, retention, and loss of thousands of customers and allows learners to put the customer centricity essentials they have learned into practice to win over those customers. It took more than two years to develop, and in 2015 we successfully launched it. During this time, we learned a great deal that we realized could also help those outside the classroom who are struggling with these issues in their organizations.

We soon decided to write a book that would be a true playbook for developing a customer-centric organization. Whereas Peter's first book, *Customer Centricity*, makes the case for moving away from a product-centric strategy to a customer-centric strategy, *The Customer Centricity Playbook* shows customer-centricity converts where to start to develop and implement a winning customer-centric strategy.

What's Next

Chapter 1 lays a foundation for the book by defining *customer centricity*, a term that is used widely but often incorrectly. In this first chapter we discuss the importance of customer heterogeneity and explain the right and wrong ways to think about CLV—a key building block for a customer-centric strategy. Chapter 2 delves into the first step in the customer journey—acquisition—and explores various strategies and tactics. We also discuss why personas and demographics are archaic customer acquisition approaches that should be retired. Chapter 3 shifts the conversation to fine-tuning retention and development activities by leveraging CLV. Chapter 4 focuses on the data analytics, technology tools, and processes that are the pillars of customer relationship management (CRM) and are all essential to customer centricity. Chapter 5 discusses the differences between traditional approaches to corporate valuation and why it is beneficial to use customer-based corporate valuation to draw a fuller picture of an organization's financial health, which will also drive specific operational decisions. Finally, chapter 6 discusses organizational transformation, culture, and leadership, which are all key to sustaining any customer-centric strategy.

Chapter 1

Setting a Strategic Course to Maximize Customer Value

I n this chapter, we provide a working definition of customer centricity that will carry through the rest of the book. We also delve into the issues of product centricity versus customer centricity, explore the concept of customer lifetime value (CLV), and take a look at Best Buy, which has transformed itself in recent years into a customer-centric success story.

Defining Customer Centricity

Despite its increased use in the world of commerce, **customer centricity** remains a tricky concept for many organizations to define or enact successfully. The problem lies in the fact that many organizations assume they're already customer centric, because they believe customer centricity is all about perfecting customer service or shifting corporate strategies to better align with the needs of their overall customer base. The term certainly *sounds* like it has something to do with making *the customer* the *central* focus of your organization. But it doesn't.

Asking what "the average customer" is worth or how *the customer* will respond to various types of products and offerings is an outdated way of thinking that fails to recognize the distinct attributes of customers on a more granular level. Their propensity to buy, their tendency to be loyal, their ways of communicating with one another, their categorically different responses to the same offers—these inherently varied qualities all affect the way they react to your company, and thus their value to your company. If you conventionally consider *the customer* as a singular, monolithic entity, then you are selling yourself (and your customers) short. More importantly, you have not yet grasped what it truly means to be customer centric.

In Peter's first book, he defined customer centricity as "a strategy that aligns the development and delivery of a company's products and services with the current and future needs of its highest valued customers in order to maximize these customers' long-term financial value to the firm."[8] Key to this definition is the idea that not all customers are created equal, which means that they don't all deserve an equal share of your organization's valuable time and resources. To be clear, this doesn't mean you should "fire" your worst customers or ignore them wholesale, but it does mean that you should know at what point you're throwing away valuable resources on customers who aren't valuable enough to deserve the level of attention you're giving them.

When someone becomes your customer, they are born to you with their own set of characteristics, categorized by preference, propensity, and potential. These traits manifest in different ways, and we refer to them collectively as **customer goodness**.

- *Preference* refers to the degree to which your offering aligns with a customer's needs and the degree to which a customer chooses your offering over a competitor's.
- *Propensity* examines the actions of your customers: their likelihood of being loyal, of referring others, of buying higher-valued offerings, and so on.
- *Potential* is the future value of each customer and what we might be leaving on the table by looking ahead; we ask ourselves, What can we do to maintain, enhance, and extract value?

Once you start breaking down customer value into these three forms of goodness (among others), you realize just how heterogeneous your customer base really is—and you can better see the opportunity to grow your business by focusing on the right customers. (We discuss customer goodness further in chapter 2.)

A truly customer-centric organization seeks to understand the inherent characteristics that make up its highest-valued customers, often leaning on modern customer relationship management (CRM) systems (which we discuss in chapter 4) to deliver the necessary insight and then—having gained newfound perspective—find and acquire other customers with similar characteristics. From a customer retention and development standpoint, knowing who your best customers are allows the limited resources within your organization to be spent more wisely on serving those customers better, thereby driving up the market value of your business.

Customer Centricity versus Product Centricity

Now that we have defined customer centricity, let's compare the concept with another common—yet floundering—business strategy: **product centricity.** Many commercial enterprises still take a product-centric approach to business, which derives value creation from a lone proposition: selling as many products and services to as many faceless, nameless customers as possible.

When companies ignore customer value in favor of being product-obsessed, they must organize around their products (or services[9]) to maximize product expertise rather than investing in strategies that will garner higher returns by seeking to acquire, retain, and develop the highest-value customers. A product-centric approach ignores customer heterogeneity and wastes valuable resources on chasing down product sales to anyone and everyone, at any cost.

For an example of product centricity's failings, look no further than shopping malls and the alarming number of store closures and bankruptcies that have happened in recent years. No retailer is immune to the bottom dropping out of their business, from small specialty stores such as Rue21, which closed a third of its stores in 2017,[10] as well as large retailers such as Macy's, which since 2016 has closed 15% of its stores, representing a loss of over 10,000 jobs.[11] Indeed, 2017 was a year most brick-and-mortars would rather forget, with almost 9,000 stores in the United States closing their doors for good.[12] This trend continues on a downward trajectory.

A number of indices have been created to track and pick over the carcasses of struggling brick and mortars, such as Bespoke Investment Group's "Death by Amazon" index. This index tracks the stocks of 62 retailers[13] and Proshares' "Decline of the Retail Store" (EMTY) exchange traded fund (ETF), which is composed of 56 retailer stocks. With a certain level of grotesqueness, EMTY is the first ETF designed to benefit from the decline of brick and mortars, making capital by shorting its very own Solactive-ProShares Bricks and Mortar Retail Store Index. Given that 70% of the stocks tracked in EMTY declined in 2017, with 25 stocks falling more than 20% in value,[14] vulturine investment tactics like this fund are reaping some tidy returns.

You may be wondering whether product centricity is to blame for such declines or whether customers are simply moving their business to online retailers with better prices. As a case study, let's look at Best Buy, a company that for a long time looked like it would go the way of CompUSA, Circuit City, and Radio Shack. Against all odds, Best Buy has managed to rebound in spectacular fashion—a recovery that is reflected in its current status as a Wall Street darling, and that can be credited to the fact that the company pivoted to a customer-centric strategy.

Best Buy: An Unlikely Customer-Centric Cinderella Story

Best Buy's stock price shot up from $10/share in December 2013 to more than $70/share at the close of 2017, indicating further robustness by gaining 50% in value in 2017 alone.[15] So how was Best Buy able to contradict most analysts' gloomy predictions that it too would go bankrupt and instead become the rare success story of a big-box retailer thriving in an Amazon era?

Figure 1.1. New York Stock Exchange Historical Market Summary, 2011–2018: Best Buy Co Inc.

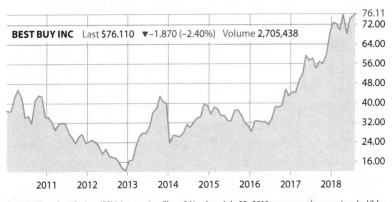

Source: "Best Buy Co Inc. (BBY) Interactive Chart," Nasdaq, July 23, 2018, www.nasdaq.com/symbol/bby /interactive-chart.

In mid-2012, the company was in an undeniable crisis, as shown in Figure 1.1. Its stock was continuing to plummet to the point where it had lost 50% of its value in six years, made worse when a scandal erupted that implicated Best Buy's most senior leadership: An investigation led by the board found that then-CEO Brian Dunn was having an inappropriate relationship with a female employee. The report also uncovered that Best Buy's founder and chair, Richard Schulze, had known about the affair and had chosen not to report it. In the wake of the investigation's findings, Dunn was fired and Schulze tendered his resignation.

The board then surprised the public when it named Hubert Joly as the new CEO. Joly, an executive from the hospitality company Carlton, had spent a decade as a business consultant at McKinsey but had absolutely no retail experience. This choice left most people scratching their heads, and many wondered whether the board's decision to hire Joly would self-sabotage Best Buy's chances of recovery.

To get a clearer assessment of the problems plaguing the company, Joly spent his first weeks visiting stores and speaking to employees. In his first report to the board, he said, "This is the most dysfunctional organization I've ever seen, but this is good news because this is self-inflicted, and so this is something we can correct."[16] He was right in saying this. But why?

In the stores, he learned about a common practice called *show-rooming*, where potential customers came to Best Buy to view a product in the flesh and would then search the internet for the cheapest provider, which in many cases was not Best Buy. Joly decided the only way to curtail this practice was to take price off the table, and thus Best Buy would be in a better position to compete head-on with the Amazons of the world. By making sure that any price offered by competitors was matched, Best Buy ensured that potential customers who came to its showrooms to view a product were not immediately lost when they did quick searches for the product on their phones and found a better offer.

Next, Joly worked to improve the online side of the business, creating a "showcase-and-ship" strategy that leveraged the 1,000-plus big-box stores to make a network of micro warehouses. This strategy allowed Best Buy to support online deliveries that rival and in many cases beat the turnaround offered by other major online retailers.[17] Why, then, didn't Joly decide to just shift the entire business online at this point?

The answer lies in an analysis of Best Buy's customer base that was originally conducted in 2010. This study found that 55% of the company's business came from women who sought more than simply the cheapest product.[18] Rather, this highly valuable customer segment wanted help from knowledgeable staff who could assist them with assessing the comparisons, purchasing ancillary products, and, in many cases, providing in-home installation. And with technology becoming increasingly complex with products that integrate multiple devices via the Internet of Things,[19] Joly also recognized an emerging demand for more expertise in product services from male and female customers alike. Indeed, smart-home integrated devices have been the fastest-growing class of customer electronics in recent years.[20]

Joly realized that by not catering to the service and support needs of women and customers in the smart-home category, Best Buy was inadvertently walking away from millions in potential sales. These customers were not simply seeking to purchase a product when they came to Best Buy, but rather to tap into staff expertise. Accordingly, the next part of Joly's strategy was to ensure continuous training of the showroom staff on all the offerings the store carried while also making sure Best Buy's GeekSquad was well equipped to provide technical support and installation. By focusing on its highest-value customers, Best Buy was able to differentiate itself from online retailers and reinvent itself in an otherwise cut-throat business. Even juggernaut Amazon recognized this smart play: Amazon tried to replicate Best Buy's GeekSquad with the launch of its own in-house smart-home installation service in mid-2017.[21]

If other retailers embrace reinvention as Best Buy has, they too could thrive in this new era of customer empowerment, in which every customer carries an entire marketplace in their pocket.

The Importance of CLV

Understanding **customer lifetime value** is the key step in developing a customer-centric strategy, yet it is frequently misunderstood in practice. Peter took a big step to move the CLV conversation forward by cofounding a predictive analytics firm, Zodiac, in 2015 to bring clarity, credibility, and high yet achievable standards to the practical calculation and deployment of CLV. As a testament to Zodiac's success in this regard, Nike bought the firm in early 2018.[22]

Our goal in this section is to help you develop the right mindset about CLV so you can leverage the insight it provides as the bedrock of your customer-centric strategy. We highlight the most important qualitative aspects of CLV and also tell you the most common mistakes people make in calculating CLV so you can avoid such pitfalls.

There are many CLV formulas in use on the internet and in marketing classes around the world, but most of these are flawed. Peter, along with Bruce Hardie, has described the collective confusion over calculating CLV in several articles.[23] It's important to understand which formulas are the most accurate and, therefore, the most useful, as well as the fundamental issues that plague the others. By understanding these distinctions, you will gain additional insight into how some fundamental customer dynamics operate and some commonly believed myths that you should avoid.

Predicting Expected CLV

CLV is a forward-looking, predictive measurement that is calculated by modeling and projecting the following:

- How long the customer relationship lasted (for churned customers) or is likely to last (for active and future customers);
- Number of transactions;
- Value of the transactions; and
- Other nonfinancial activities the customer may engage in (e.g., visits to website, willingness to try other products, posting ratings and reviews about the company's products, and/or referring other prospective customers)

Remember that for any current and yet-to-be-acquired customers representing future cashflows, CLV is still based on a *prediction*, as there's no ironclad way of knowing the actual number of periods they'll remain customers, how many purchases they will make, and so forth. With that said, it's important to call this calculation what it really is: expected CLV, or **ECLV**. Hereafter, for clarity and convenience, we refer to the concept of customer lifetime value as *CLV*, but we do want to call out the importance in your own organization of knowing when you are speaking about ECLV versus CLV.

CLV is defined as "the present value of the future cashflows (profit) attributed to the customer relationship,"[24] with *future* being the operative word. Therefore, to calculate CLV, you must project the length of time that customers will remain active while recognizing the probabilistic uncertainty around this number. Likewise, you must make projections about the other behaviors of interest, such as, How many transactions will the customer make during their lifetime? and How large will these transactions be? These are critical quantities, but the manner in which you determine them—and the confidence you can have in those calculations—depends on the status of the customer.

CLV Mistake Number 1: Failing to Account for the Status of the Customer

The first set of issues with many CLV formulas relates to the status of the customer. To determine a customer's status, you ask the following kinds of questions: Is this a prospect we will likely acquire in the future? Did we just acquire them and thus lack any historical information about them? Have they been recently active or have they likely departed? Based on the status of the customer, different formulas should be used to calculate CLV that take into account whether you're predicting the value of active and future customers or doing a retrospective calculation on already-churned—lost—customers. Frustratingly, as no future relationship is set in stone, the only category of customer for which you can accurately calculate CLV is those who have already churned.

Of course, these customers are not at all representative of the overall customer base, so while you should embrace the certainty provided by these ex-customers—and leverage data about them to build models that better predict how your existing and future customers will perform—you must also acknowledge and attempt to quantify the uncertainty associated with the still-active (and not-yet-acquired) ones. There is tremendous opportunity to mine the information about past customers to help shore up your predictions about the value of current and future customers. Again, when mining data about past customers, ensure that you don't just lump them into one bucket, but recognize their heterogeneity. (We talk more about customer heterogeneity in chapter 2.)

CLV Mistake Number 2: Forgetting to Distinguish Contractual from Noncontractual Customers

Unless you are clairvoyant, for noncontractual enterprises it is impossible to be absolutely certain that a particular customer is still active. It's relatively simple to make this projection for a subscription-based or "contractual" business model, such as a weekly meal kit or a gym membership, because a client must renew their contract in order to stay or cancel it if they opt to leave. But what about noncontractual enterprises? Consider online retailers, coffee shops, and hotel chains; in these settings, if a customer hasn't been active for a while, it can be difficult to tell whether they're gone for good or will reemerge at some point. The notion of a "retention rate," which makes sense in a contractual setting, is meaningless here—it is impossible to know how many noncontractual customers are even still alive, so we'll never know if we truly retained them. For these reasons, no single CLV formula can be used across contractual and noncontractual businesses.

To avoid the miscalculations outlined in these first two common CLV mistakes, we recommend using a specific set of formulas that consider whether the business model is contractual or noncontractual, and whether the customer is current, newly acquired, or a future asset. For contractual businesses where attrition is observable, retention rates should be used in the CLV calculation, but since noncontractual firms can't know for sure when a customer has left, we don't use retention rates in that calculation.

Calculating CLV for noncontractual businesses is further complicated because the flow of transactions is very different than in the contractual setting. In the latter case, payments tend to arise at regular intervals (e.g., via monthly cable bills) and the payment amounts tend to be fairly consistent over time. But in the noncontractual setting, payment times and amounts vary widely. The "binge buying" that takes place at certain times of year (e.g., back to school) or around certain life events (e.g., moving houses or getting married) leads to highly irregular purchase patterns. Noncontractual businesses have to work much harder to make such predictions, and they cannot rely on the contractual models as a quick and dirty approximation. The estimates will likely be way off for each component of behavior and thus for CLV as a whole.

CLV Mistake Number 3: Believing That Customer Retention Rates Remain Constant over Time

The third misstep in most CLV formulas for contractual businesses is the incorrect assumption that retention rates will remain constant over time among a cohort of customers who were all acquired during the same period. This problematic shortcut is likely being overlooked because there aren't many differences when retention rates are measured in the aggregate across multiple cohorts. But according to Peter and Bruce, taking this shortcut will lead to the *wrong* CLV calculation:

> The relatively constant retention rates observed in the company-reported summaries are in fact a result of aggregation across cohorts of customers. New customers (with relatively low retention rates) are being averaged in with existing customers, thereby masking the pattern (of increasing retention rates over time) that we would likely see for any given cohort by itself.[25]

The authors provide further justifications for why these shortcuts should be avoided in the 2010 *Marketing Science* article "Customer-Base Valuation in a Contractual Setting: The Perils of Ignoring Heterogeneity," which is based on their study of what happens when these cohort-level dynamics are ignored. Peter and Bruce offer the following conclusions on the inaccuracies related to overlooking varying retention rates in a cohort over time:

> [Our analysis] finds that valuations performed using an aggregate retention rate underestimate the true value of the customer base by the order of 25%–50% in standard settings.[26]

Figure 1.2. Realistic versus Constant Customer Retention Rate

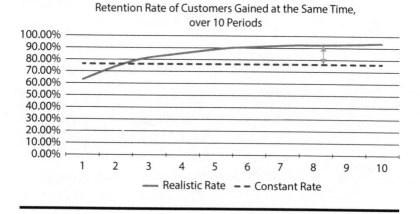

To help illustrate the difference between a constant retention rate and one that takes into account a more realistic, variable retention rate for the cohort over time, let's take a look at Figure 1.2 and what happens over 10 periods for a group of customers who were acquired in the same period. The dotted line in the graph represents a constant retention rate of 76%, which was calculated by taking an average of the projected retention rates over 10 periods. The solid line represents a more realistic trend of how many original customers are still with this firm in each period.

As you can see, the significant gap between the two rates reveals why using the constant retention rate leads to, in this case, many fewer customers considered in the CLV calculation by the end of period 10. And the gap would obviously continue to grow over time, further underestimating the future value of the cohort.

The explanation behind this substantial gap is often not appreciated by managers who fail to "celebrate heterogeneity," as we call it. It is generally not the case that each individual customer is becoming more loyal or locked in over time, which is what many people would conclude from this kind of graph. Instead, we are seeing a shakeout due to heterogeneity: The subset of customers who stay with the company for several periods are likely to be better customers and will therefore continue to stay longer than the original cohort as a whole.[27] Such behaviors should inform investment strategies. In a mature cohort, investment shouldn't be wasted on retaining already sticky customers; rather, investments should be spent figuring out ways to create and extract further value from this set of customers and to find more customers like them.

Similar issues arise in the noncontractual setting, but they are impossible to see and measure directly owing to the latent attrition process described above. Even when they are latent, attrition propensities vary greatly across customers, leading to observable patterns in the data that are more a reflection of cross-customer differences than dynamics within a specific person over time.

CLV Mistake Number 4: Your Customers Aren't Normal

When we ask our students to describe how customers vary by CLV, many respond immediately by invoking the normal distribution (or a bell curve), which looks like Figure 1.3.

Figure 1.3. The Mythical Bell Curve of CLV

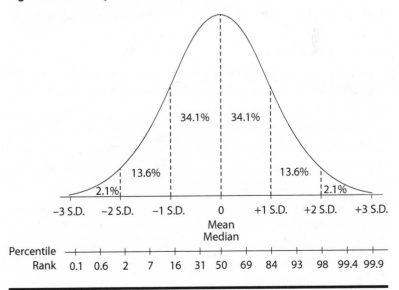

Figure 1.4. The Reality of CLV Distribution

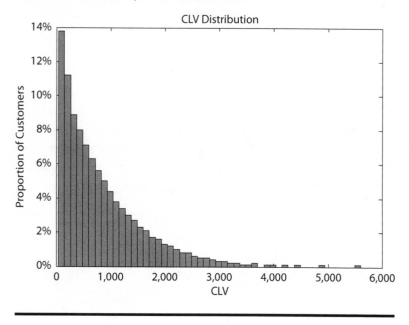

This answer arises as a knee-jerk response to almost any statistical question because of the ubiquity of normal distribution in introductory statistics courses. If this trend were true, life would be easy: We would rid ourselves of the clearly distinguishable left tail of low-value customers and focus on everyone else. But when it comes to CLV, your customers aren't normal—normally distributed, that is.

What we see in reality is a distribution of CLV that looks like the graph in Figure 1.4, with lower-value customers making up the largest proportion. As CLV increases, there are fewer and fewer customers, but this right tail extends out a long way. This means that your modal customer can be found toward the lower end of the CLV scale, and thus efforts to prune them out, if done wrong, would have sweeping strategic implications. Essentially, when it comes to "firing" customers, choosing accurately is difficult, and there's much to lose by choosing poorly.

This more realistic view also lines up with the famous "80:20 rule"—that is, the bottom 80% of customers bring in only 20% of the total value. This guideline turns out to be fairly accurate in many cases. Some industries are less concentrated: For instance, grocery products often show up as a 60:20 ratio.[28] But in other industries, such as the revenues arising from freemium games, the numbers are extraordinarily concentrated—more like a 90:5 ratio. Regardless of the precise numbers, as long as there is a meaningful degree of concentration within customers—which is the same thing as heterogeneity across them—the value distribution will look more like Figure 1.4.

CLV "Mistake" Number 5: Beyond Dollars and Cents

We use quotation marks around "mistake" in the name of this error because our final words of caution aren't about a mistake per se, but rather a common omission. Most CLV calculations are purely financial. While that's appropriate for many business settings, there are some businesses where limiting your CLV to finances is inadequate.

For instance, in industries such as healthcare, the idea of predicting the CLV of various customers carries with it some obvious ethical and legal considerations. What are the implications if the best customers are the least healthy ones? Perhaps in the context of CLV in healthcare, the word *lifetime* should be taken literally, because any life-extending measures surely create meaningful value. Dwight McNeill touches on this idea in his book *A Framework for Applying Analytics in Healthcare: What Can Be Learned from the Best Practices in Retail, Banking, Politics, and Sports.* He explains:

> What if lifetime value were actually about the length of a life? What if health plans/systems were rewarded for producing longer and more functional lives? And what if there were financial incentives for this lifetime value rather than the production of more services? So the concept of lifetime value all turns on the value orientation. Using analytical methods for tracking people longitudinally over a lifetime would put the focus on

long-term improvements in healthcare. Also, CLV analytics can be used to improve health for everyone, to lift all boats, and by doing so can add value to the bottom line and fortify the brand through its integrity and dedication of purpose to the health and well-being of all customers.[29]

You can see McNeill's point at work in retail pharmacy chains. Most of them use a traditional loyalty program that gives you points based on your spending in the store, but some also have a separate "wellness" reward scheme in which you get credit for buying healthy products or doing other health-enhancing activities, such as getting a flu shot or a blood-pressure test.

A similar scenario can arise in financial services, where customers who frequently incur overdraft fees may have a higher lifetime value—in purely financial terms—than those who don't incur overdraft fees. But, once again, this system misses the point of customer centricity and what we mean by "value." Other such examples abound:

- Member-driven community organizations, such as religious institutions and charities, shouldn't look only at donations but should also account for volunteering efforts and other positive types of engagement.
- Media firms shouldn't look only at fees paid for subscriptions and content consumption but should also consider users' sharing and promoting their content on social media.
- Firms in many industries should monitor referral behavior as an important source of value, above and beyond the financial value gained from the referring customers.

These omissions are easy to understand since it's much harder to track these auxiliary behaviors compared with payments. But the value created by these nonfinancial activities can be substantial, and the presence of these behaviors may be a useful indicator of "customer goodness" that can help firms better identify the kinds of customers they want to work extra hard to attract and retain.

Chapter Summary

- Customer centricity aligns the development and delivery of a company's products and services with the current and future needs of its highest-value customers while also recognizing—and celebrating—customer heterogeneity. This strategy maximizes these customers' long-term value to the firm.
- Product centricity is the practice of selling as many products and services as possible to as many anonymous customers as possible—in other words, the exact opposite of customer centricity. Product centricity is an outmoded, ineffective business strategy.
- CLV is a predictive measurement calculated by modeling and projecting the length of a customer relationship, the number of transactions a customer will make, the value of the transactions, and any nonfinancial activities a customer may engage in. Many firms make mistakes when calculating ECLV, but this measurement is essential to a successful customer-centric strategy.

Chapter 2

Customer Acquisition and Growing Your Best Customer Base

As we mentioned in the introduction, customer-centric firms recognize that there are three key tactics used to grow their most valuable customer base: customer acquisition, customer retention, and customer development. A central goal of this book is to help train your eye to see these tactics as three distinct, yet deeply intertwined, activities.

This chapter focuses on **customer acquisition** and provides strategies to help you maximize the value of the customers you acquire. Customer acquisition signifies the beginning of the customer's lifetime. As noted earlier, you often have more control over the kinds of customers you bring in as opposed to trying to change them after they've been acquired. We should point out that this statement runs in direct opposition to a common but misguided piece of business advice: It costs [X] times more to acquire a new customer than to retain an existing one, so you should focus on the ones you already have. This traditional volume-oriented (and cost-minimizing) perspective arises from product-centric thinking as opposed to a more long-term, CLV-oriented, customer-centric approach.

Recognizing that not all customers are created equal gives you the opportunity to view acquisition as a truly strategic weapon, and not just a tactical exercise that sees generic customers as the fuel for a product-driven strategy.

Amazon's Acquisition Strategy

When Jeff Bezos launched Amazon in 1994, why did he decide to sell books through an online marketplace? Books are heavy, are expensive to ship, and generate paltry margins, and—let's be honest—Americans aren't exactly known for being bookish en masse. In actuality, Bezos's business strategy had nothing to do with the products but rather with the customers who bought them. He recognized that those interested in purchasing books are relatively affluent, and thus sales to these customers provided infinite opportunities to mine information about the behaviors and untapped potential of a highly valuable segment of online customers—which is a reasonable proxy for CLV. As we discussed in chapter 1, nailing this concept is core to a winning customer-centric strategy. With this key insight, Amazon was able to light the path to finding and acquiring throngs of other online customers with similarly high lifetime values. You know what happened next: Bezos's predication for the future of the internet was spot-on, and his gamble to quit a lucrative position at a New York City hedge fund to start his online bookstore paid off—big time! Amazon is now the world's largest online retailer[30] with a net worth of over $430 billion[31] (for comparison, that is almost twice the value of Walmart).

But we often forget that Amazon wasn't *always* the one to beat. Bezos founded Amazon in the dawn of the internet after becoming intrigued with the exponential growth of online usage and sales. A year after founding Amazon, he was in Chicago at a national publishing conference, where he hung a sign at Amazon's booth boldly proclaiming that the company was "Earth's Biggest Bookstore." This daring statement caught the attention of Roger Doeren, chief operating officer of Rainy Day Books, a Kansas-based independent bookstore. As reported by the *New Yorker*, Doeren was puzzled by this claim and questioned Bezos on where, specifically, his bookstore was located. Bezos replied "Cyberspace!" and then went on to say that he

intended to sell books as a way of gathering data on affluent, educated shoppers. The books would be priced close to cost, in order to increase sales volume. After collecting data on millions of customers, Amazon could figure out how to sell everything else dirt cheap on the Internet.[32]

Many people were skeptical that Bezos would be able to break even, much less make a profit. Indeed, many business analysts at the time asked why Bezos decided to start an online bookstore during a time when publishers were in a panic over shrinking book sales.[33] As that early conversation with Doeren reveals, Bezos was looking for something—anything—that could be shipped without breaking and would reap bounties of customer data. This strategy was brilliant because Bezos knew that once Amazon had gathered a massive cache of customer data, he'd have a winning formula for pushing past his gateway drug of book sales and be able to sell everything else over the internet. And in doing so, he created a winning company based on customer centricity.

Understanding Customer Goodness and Celebrating Customer Diversity

Customer centricity seeks to understand which characteristics are most closely associated with the lifetime value of a customer. This concept can be explained by thinking of each customer as having been born with a degree of **customer goodness**, a set of baked-in propensities that manifest themselves in customers' preferences and translate into customers' potential value, as discussed in chapter 1. To capitalize on customer goodness, you should focus on certain likelihoods, such as how long a customer could potentially remain your customer, how much they are likely to spend throughout their life cycle with your company, and so forth.

This basic idea isn't new—it was first popularized in the 1996 book *The Loyalty Effect* by Frederick Reichheld.[34] The "loyalty effect" presaged the idea of customer goodness by suggesting that top customers rewarded a firm in multiple ways—for example, they stayed longer, spent more, were cheaper to serve, and were good sources of referrals. Back in 1996 this was more of a conceptual idea than a practical one. But today we have the data, analytics, and technology to bring this idea to life at the most granular level. Your objective is to make this general idea of customer goodness—and each of its underlying behavioral propensities—as actionable as possible while also fully appreciating how the propensities vary across customers.

There are many propensities that can lead to higher CLV, such as a customer's predilection to make repeat or higher-value purchases or their likelihood to evangelize your business and refer others your way. As with the loyalty effect, the basic idea of customer goodness is that these propensities tend to be linked at the customer level: If a customer stays, the customer spends. But each customer also has a heterogeneous makeup when it comes to the linkages in their personal propensities. A customer being good in one respect does not necessarily mean they are good in *every* respect. For example, one customer might prefer your product over your competitors' and thus have a low propensity to leave, but this same customer might not have much need for what you're offering, so they have a lower propensity to purchase, which manifests in a less frequent repeat-purchase cycle. Another customer might be similar to the first in that they too prefer your product over your competitors', but they have a *greater* need for what you're offering than that other customer, resulting in a more frequent repeat-purchase cycle. Given the different propensities of these two customers, which one has the higher CLV? This question is what every customer-centric firm must answer when mining and analyzing data for current and past customers.

Even though a customer is born with baseline propensities, they aren't *completely* set in stone; you can develop these propensities to improve the customer's overall value to your firm. Smart investments such as premium services and loyalty programs often help foster customers' CLV. Likewise, if your brand reputation gets a boost, some customers may develop higher propensities than their original baseline to stay and spend as a result. In contrast, if a client has a terrible experience with your customer service department, leading to the customary "I demand to speak to your manager!" before escalating into furious threats to take their business elsewhere, this customer is much more likely to follow through with that threat and leave at some point.

This is all to say that investing in retention and development is also crucial for maintaining and improving customer goodness. We'll dive into these issues in the next chapter, but here we want to make sure you recognize that these are not the *only* relevant factors in customer goodness. You need to make sure that you're acquiring pretty good customers in the first place.

Fishing for the Best Customers

At this point, nearly every marketer on Earth has used a fishing metaphor to describe customer acquisition. We are no exception. The metaphor is a good one, so you'll have to forgive us for not thinking of something new.

You're fishing out on the open ocean (i.e., the marketplace), hopeful you'll catch at least a few big fish (i.e., customers). You have a crew with you; some are using spears while others are working the nets. In this metaphor, the crew represents your sales and marketing teams. The people with spears are engaged in direct sales and marketing, while those with nets are working the indirect angle (e.g., using external agencies or mass marketing efforts). The crew members with spears are naturally far choosier about when they thrust their spear into the waters, because it takes a lot of effort and can easily miss—each attempt had better catch a good-quality fish. Those with nets are less picky because once the nets are submerged, they're fishing blind, but they also know their chances of pulling up a substantial catch are pretty good. But whether their haul includes a good mix of big fish is unclear.

So what happens when you deploy a fleet of boats, some with a team using spears and others equipped with nets? You get to decide where on the open ocean to send these teams to fish.

As with the ocean, there is great variability in the marketplace with respect to which types of customers are swimming where. As previously described, we call this **heterogeneity**. Conventional sales and marketing teams focus on customer heterogeneity more from a quantity standpoint than a quality one, so they tend to focus their energy on finding spots in the marketplace that reap the most new customers at the lowest possible cost. Many of the traditional customer acquisition "dashboard" metrics, such as conversion rates and cost per acquisition, reflect this kind of thinking.

Customer-centric sales and marketing teams' primary objective is different. They want to find where the highest-value customers are likely to be swimming and direct more of their efforts to catching better customers. But that doesn't mean they use only the spears: It is important to ensure that they're getting an adequate number of new customers to fill their sales channel, even if they can't all be whales. Thus, a truly customer-centric captain will deploy spears to the best places to catch the best fish while also relying on nets to ensure that the business will continue to run smoothly. Finding this balance is challenging but critical.

In Peter's first book, he spoke briefly about this balancing act under the label of the "Paradox of Customer Centricity."[35] Essentially, the more you obsess over finding the best customers (by throwing spears), the more you need the nets to keep the business afloat. Customer-centric firms also recognize that as they go back to the same place to fish for new customers, the average quality of customers in that area will tend to worsen over time. In this regard, time is essential to defining an effective acquisition strategy: As the average CLV of customers decreases, it may make sense to shift to using a less precise and cheaper acquisition tactic. (We discuss the difference between broad, selective, direct, and indirect strategies and tactics in the next section of this chapter.)

Admittedly, when the fish-customer is caught, this metaphor blows up, because soon after you pull a real fish out of the water, it dies. For any vegetarian and vegan folks who have hated reading this chapter so far, you'll be delighted to hear that our fish-customers live on, and the fisherman-marketing-and-sales-people will be doing everything in their power to ensure that their recently caught fish-customers have a long life!

Strategies and Tactics Used to Acquire New Customers

Marketers use two main types of strategies to draw in new customers: broad and selective. A **broad strategy** casts a wide net in order to gain lots of new customers. A **selective strategy**, on the other hand, requires the precision targeting of a spear to bring in fewer but higher-quality customers. Beyond these broad strategic objectives, marketers also have two distinct categories of tactics for customer acquisition: **direct**, for known prospects, and **indirect**, for unknown prospects. We discuss each of these categories on their own and then show you how permutations of the broader strategies and narrower tactics can be put into practice.

Broad Acquisition Strategy

At first glance, a broad marketing strategy might seem antithetical to customer centricity, since one of the primary goals of customer centricity is to bring in the highest-valued customers. But "spearing" is not the best acquisition strategy for all situations. Think about a new business or new product launch: In these early stages, companies must prove that there is a demand for their offering, so a broad strategy makes sense—filling the sales pipeline and stimulating network effects is often the top priority. Casting a wide net is also a good strategy for companies that are selling something that doesn't get a lot of repeat purchases, such as new homes or LASIK eye correction surgery. The broad approach is also perfect for those companies faced with really low customer satisfaction that's causing high churn rates, because new customers need to be continually acquired to balance out the many who are leaving.

(A brief side note: Consider this last example. If a firm is losing potentially high-value customers at high rates because something it's doing is lousy, like customer service, there is no chance of achieving a customer base with high CLV. Acquisition addiction is *not* the path to customer centricity, as we will discuss in chapter 5.)

Selective Acquisition Strategy

A selective strategy is best for companies that need to be pickier about which customers they're acquiring. Maybe the company has capacity constraints, or the switching costs are high so the company knows the average customer will be with it for a long time. Ivy League schools, such as the University of Pennsylvania, are highly selective about which students are admitted, and therefore, a broad approach, like taking out a billboard on the Schuylkill Expressway, isn't a well-matched acquisition strategy for the school. Private banking is another great example in this category, where customers are invited to join, and in return will receive special, white-glove treatment. For this offering, the bank must be exclusive with who it chooses as customers because it can accommodate only so many.

So far, we've used edge cases to describe the types of businesses and situations that might require a broad versus a selective strategy. However, most companies will do best to use a *blended* approach. You should run experiments within your organization to test the right balance of this mix of broad and selective—specifically, use the "spear" to ensure you haven't missed any potentially high-value customers and the "net" to backfill your sales channel. Also keep in mind that there are some synergies/complementarities across the two approaches: The insights gained by the spear throwers might be able to help the net folks identify better places to cast out, and vice versa.

Using Both Strategies and Tactics

As we said at the beginning of the chapter, broad and selective marketing strategies are often used in conjunction with two distinct

Figure 2.1. Types of Acquisition Strategies and Tactics

	STRATEGY	
	BROAD	**SELECTIVE**
DIRECT	• Lead Generation • Telemarketing • "Detailing"	• Profiling/Scoring Models • "Lookalike" Methods • Social-Network Neighbor Methods
INDIRECT	• Mass Marketing • Random Seeding • Word-of-Mouth	• Influential Seeding • Referrals • 2nd Degree Targeting

(row label, vertical: **TACTICS**)

categories of tactics for customer acquisition: direct (when you know who the prospects are) and indirect (when prospects are unknown). Think back to the fishing metaphor: throwing a spear pairs a selective strategy with a direct tactic. Conversely, throwing a net is a broad approach using an indirect tactic. But other combinations are logical too, resulting in the tidy-looking 2×2 matrix in Figure 2.1[36] (because we all know how much business school professors *love* their 2×2s!).

Now that you have a basic grasp of these strategies and tactics, let's look a little more closely at each pairing.

Direct-Broad Acquisition Approach

The direct-broad approach targets specific individual customers, but little is known about these potential leads. Here, companies develop or purchase a list of potential prospects and then decide which ones to target.[37] Though the names, addresses, phone numbers, and other high-level details are provided, little else is known about these leads. Examples of how these leads are reached broadly following this approach include telemarketing, Google marketing, and canvassing.

Direct-Selective Acquisition Approach

In the direct-selective approach, marketers usually use two sets of models to describe and then find good customers. They start with their own datasets and run *profiling models* that help identify the characteristics that best distinguish high-CLV customers from lesser ones. These could include demographics (which we discuss later in this chapter), interactions with the product or the firm, and so on. Once marketers have developed the right profile, they turn to external prospect lists and *scoring models* to determine which prospects seem to most closely fit that profile. One popular method of implementing this process is by using the "Lookalike Audiences" service that Facebook offers[38] or other equivalent services through Google and other such platforms. Today's rich datasets and "real-time" analytical tools make this kind of exercise easy. It can be powerful, but it can also become less effective over time when the firm "overfishes" certain waters.

In our socially connected era, it is now possible to profile and score based less on characteristics about each individual customer and more about the neighborhood in the overall "social graph" where they reside. One of the first studies in the marketing science field to quantitatively prove that product adoption is positively affected by linkage to an existing customer drew the following conclusions:

(1) "Network neighbors"—those consumers linked to a prior customer—adopt the service at a rate 3–5 times greater than baseline groups selected by the best practices of the firm's marketing team. In addition, analyzing the network allows the firm to acquire new customers who otherwise would have fallen through the cracks, because they would not have been identified

based on traditional attributes. (2) Statistical models, built with a very large amount of geographic, demographic and prior purchase data, are significantly and substantially improved by including network information. (3) More detailed network information allows the ranking of the network neighbors so as to permit the selection of small sets of individuals with very high probabilities of adoption.[39]

Indirect-Broad Acquisition Approach

Good old-fashioned mass marketing is a prime example of an indirect-broad approach. This approach is all about casting the widest net to reach as many (unidentifiable) customers as possible. Traditionally, this approach brings to mind TV ads, billboards, and sponsorship activities—mass advertising where a company has taken painstaking care to craft the perfect marketing message about why its product is the best. But often there are other forces in the marketplace, where word gets out about a product in ways that, for better or worse, the company has no control over.

Indirect-Selective Acquisition Approach

In the indirect-selective approach, companies look for customers who have something in common with their existing high-value customers, but the company doesn't necessarily know who the candidate prospects are—in other words, there is no list of prospects to match up with. The classic case is referral, where businesses ask customers to bring in a friend or colleague. Referred customers deserve special recognition for several reasons:

- The cost is often far less for acquiring referred customers than the overhead involved with acquiring customers via other channels.
- A referred customer also tells you something about the customer who did the referring. These helpful brand

ambassadors are more likely to have a higher customer goodness, and thus a better CLV.

- The marketing research tells us that referred customers are often good customers, which translates into them having preferable propensities, such as higher retention.[40]

Referred customers are not always commonplace, but attracting them and rewarding the customers who referred them should be part of any customer-centric strategy.

Another indirect-selective approach is influential seeding. This approach targets nodes within a network, seeding influencers with information about a product, and depending on the *expected force*[41] of the seed node, information may or may not spread to neighboring nodes. Here, marketers take advantage of the already natural influencing effect that happens among proximate nodes where information spreads organically outward from seeded nodes to their neighbors, then to the neighbors' neighbors, and so on. Indeed, this pattern of behavior is inherent to every imaginable natural and manufactured system. This ubiquity helps us in the marketing sphere because we can draw from a rich body of research that studies the dynamics at play in influential seeding and networks in general.

In the marketing science world, some of the most groundbreaking work has come from scholars in Israel who have been studying different kinds of social seeding strategies—for example, *support-the-strong*, *support-the-weak*, and *uniform* strategies—for their effectiveness when a new product is launched in different social network settings. A novel finding in this study was that the effectiveness of these strategies changes depending on the costs to enter the region. When entry costs are low,

> strategies that disperse marketing efforts (such as uniform or support-the-weak) perform better, in terms of the net present value (NPV) of number of adopters. This finding runs counter to conventional wisdom in international marketing. [On the other hand], the higher the entry costs into a region, or the fixed

periodic operation costs in a region, the better support-the-strong strategy becomes.[42]

Why You Should Be Wary of Demographics and Personas

So far, we've talked a lot about identifying the characteristics of good customers and using those features as the basis for future customer acquisition activities. We have provided strategies for identifying those qualities, and now we would like to offer a word of caution about how *not* to identify those qualities: by using demographics and personas. To be blunt, we see these measures as antiquated and, more importantly, deeply flawed.

Consider the old parable:

> A police officer sees a drunk searching for something under a lamppost, and asks him what he's looking for. The drunk says he's lost his keys, and the officer takes pity on him and starts helping him look. After five minutes of looking, the officer says, "Are you sure you lost your keys here?"
>
> "No," the drunk replies. "I lost them in the park."
>
> "Then why are you searching over here?" the officer asks.
>
> The drunk looks at him blearily for a moment, then shrugs: "It's brighter over here."

This parable is also known as the "streetlight effect," a form of observational bias that causes people to look for things wherever it is easiest to see them.[43] This idea is applicable to many demographic-based marketing practices.

Demographics

Back in the early days of modern marketing (think late 1940s and 1950s), businesses didn't have readily available, reliable data for analyzing customers. So when **demographic segmentation** was developed, it was a huge breakthrough: For the first time, marketers could look at data and say, "Whoa, customers can be different from each other, and we can understand those differences!"

An early example of this occurred in 1947, when Chevrolet became one of the first automobile companies to launch an ad campaign aimed specifically at women.[44] Before then, marketers assumed that car purchasing was a male affair. But demographic data segmented by gender quickly disproved this myth, showing that women played a significant role in the automobile selection process too. In Chevy's new campaign, their marketers decided to craft ads that emphasized the qualities the company *believed* would attract women to its product: safety, convenience, family friendliness, and stylishness. To seal the deal, they enlisted Dinah Shore as the campaign's spokeswoman, an up-and-coming singer and television entertainer who was witty and beautiful and oozed Southern charm. (Interesting aside: This association launched Shore as one of the first TV personalities to become synonymous with a product.[45])

Chevy couldn't have chosen a better personality for this campaign. Shore was on a meteoric rise to national fame during this time, and her endorsement of Chevy helped sell massive quantities of automobiles. Americans adored her in the same way they love Oprah and Ellen DeGeneres today. For years, when Shore opened and closed her primetime show, she sang the Chevy jingle, an earworm that became known nationally, even becoming an iconic symbol of American patriotism: "See the USA in your Chevrolet. America is asking you to call. Drive your Chevrolet through the USA. America's the greatest land of all." The campaign reaped massive returns, with the "Queen of Chevy" *driving* millions of car sales for the company [46] (thank you—we'll be here all week!).

This early example of demographic advertising sounds like a marketing success story, but looking through a customer-centric lens, it really isn't. While it's commendable that the auto industry *finally* recognized that women bring value to the table, this campaign made the common mistake of thinking that all customers from the same demographic group want the same things in a product, and by extension, these customers all have the same potential value. As we've discussed, this assumption is wrong, and often costly to a business.

In the decades that followed, marketing became all about demographics. Not because demographics were all that great, mind you—they weren't—but because demographics were what marketers could get their hands on. You might be thinking, "Surely we aren't doing the same thing today, right?" Wrong. Every time you hear a marketing strategy targeting, say, the 18–34 male sector (or, dare we say it, *millennials*), that's demographic thinking at work. Not only is it a poor way to drive an effective acquisition strategy, but even for existing customers, it's relatively unusual to find demographic segments that separate customers in terms of overall value.

Fast-forward to present day and Toyota's recent marketing campaign for its new Camry. Toyota produced four ads, one each for African Americans, Hispanics, Asian Americans, and "transcultural mainstream." Which ad will you see? Well, that depends entirely on your ethnicity, of course! Given that we now know how suboptimal demographics are in terms of CLV, why has our industry continued to invest so many resources in advertising based on demographic data? Well, because *it's brighter over here.*

Usually, variation of CLV within demographic buckets is far greater than the differences across them. Sure, the mean CLV across buyers in a particular category may be higher for, say, older people versus younger people, but these differences—even if statistically significant—are relatively inconsequential compared with the vast differences within each group. Means are meaningless unless you also take the variance into account, and customer centricity is a celebration of variance.

Personas, a.k.a. Demographics on Steroids

That brings us to **personas**. Personas are a much more holistic concept than straight demographics, attitudes, or even behavioral metrics. What's not to like about the idea of being able to put a face to a customer segment? It's easy to think of marketing to Harriet

Housewife and to compare her needs with those of Working Wanda or Carpool Carla. Managers just love it; there's something intuitive about putting these cartoon characters up on a whiteboard and thinking about which ones you want to focus your acquisition efforts on.

As a result, managers and marketers behave as if these personas are a reasonable and adequate representation of their customer base. But these personas are essentially just shorthand for the demographic data they already have—demographics on steroids, so to speak. From a researcher's perspective, personas are another way of categorizing people based on surface-level characteristics that, in most cases, don't have a whole lot to do with a customer's true future value. If you want to actually gain insights into what your customer's spending habits are, how much value they contribute to your company, or any other revenue-centric data point, demographics are the wrong tool. That's a job for CLV.

Of course, even in CLV analysis, we still must profile our segments. But a customer-centric approach to segmentation is polar opposite to that of traditional marketers, who tend to start with predetermined segments (often based on demographics/personas) and ask, "Which ones seem most attractive for selling our products?" By contrast, the customer-centric marketer starts with individual-level CLVs and then asks, What are the characteristics that make our top customers different from our bottom customers? This is a key distinction in mindset as well as practice.

Admittedly, some demographic qualities may pop out during analysis, becoming important variables as we distinguish these customers into groups. A group of "top customers" may share certain qualities, even though the group itself is defined by its lifetime value. Ironically, this analysis can lead you to something that looks an awful lot like a persona. Thus, if you use CLV and behavioral models to create composites of high-value customers, the end results *could* be viewed as personas, but these results would not be nearly as tight and exclusive as persona-based marketing usually suggests. Many of the people in that segment might share common traits, but there would also be other customers within that group who don't fit neatly into the persona model.

Reverse-Engineering Personas with CLV

Knowing now that CLV analysis sometimes results in semi-personas invites the question: Can CLV be used to create *better* personas? Technically, yes, although with some serious caveats.

Let's say a company wanted to use CLV to create representative customer segments for different value levels. Generally speaking, these groups will be so demographically diverse that no clear persona would emerge. Some groups, however, will have a lot in common. Perhaps their highest-CLV segment has many college-educated women in their mid-30s who make $200,000 a year. Is that enough to justify creating a persona called "Professional Pam"?

Perhaps, but there's going to be a lot of noise and randomness within that group. Those customers won't fit as well into that persona, and some may have nothing at all in common with it. By trying to capture Professional Pam, the company may start to exclude other customers who are just as important in terms of the value they provide.

If a company is absolutely set on using personas, the best bet is to start with a CLV-based foundation. There's no better tool for creating more accurate customer models that can provide insights for winning new customers, developing new products, and informing the frontline sales force. But we'd also caution that company to be careful, because relying on personas—even thoughtfully created ones—can easily lead you astray.

CLV also shows us that the demographic assumptions behind personas are notoriously transient. Traditional, backward-looking analysis tools rarely reflect this, but CLV allows you to see these shifts as they happen. That's another reason to avoid investing too heavily in personas: By the time your graphic designer was able to deliver cartoon illustrations of "Big-Spending Bonnie" and "Deal-Hunting Donna," that persona might already be outdated, sending both of you right back to the drawing board.

Shifting to Direct

Acquisition strategies based on demographics and personas rely on perfecting indirect approaches to marketing—those represented in the bottom half of the Figure 2.1 matrix. Sometimes demographic targeting is aimed at being as broadly appealing as possible and other times at being more selective; either way, this approach is essential to *indirect* tactics. For whatever reasons, marketers haven't budged much from this mindset yet, even though they really should. We live in a time when specific information about individual customers is easy to obtain and analyze and is inexpensive to store (as we'll discuss in chapter 4). This means the world is becoming more direct all the time. And with these changing times, marketing managers and executives should be shifting resources from the bottom quadrants to the top to match this new reality.

Chapter Summary

- Firms must take into account "customer goodness"—a set of baked-in propensities that manifest themselves in customers' preferences and translate into customers' potential value—when putting customer acquisition strategies into practice.
- Customer-centric marketers use a mixture of broad and selective strategies as well as direct and indirect tactics for acquiring customers.
- Demographics and personas are ineffective tools for segmenting and marketing to customers, because these approaches tend to fall victim to the "streetlight effect"—a form of observational bias.
- In the age of digital insights, when specific information about individual customers is easy to collect, analyze, and store, companies need to be thinking of moving to more direct approaches to customer acquisition.

Chapter 3

Using Customer Centricity to Tune Retention and Development Tactics

Once a customer has been successfully acquired, the company must shift its focus to ensuring that the newly acquired customer grows and maintains their future value for as long as possible. There are two distinct yet deeply intertwined tactics that need to happen with active customers: customer **retention** and customer **development**. Retention tactics work to ensure the customer stays, while development tactics focus on ways to increase the value of existing customers.

When it comes to retaining and developing active customers, it is critical to deploy retention and development tactics to maximize the CLV of your existing and future customers. On a macro level, growing CLV requires the acquisition of a good-sized set of high-value customers. As we discussed in chapter 1, your customers are born to you with a baseline propensity to stay or leave, and to purchase. It's up to you to nudge the baseline customer-loyalty propensity by making sure your best customers don't walk out the door from one too many sour interactions with customer service or a mismatch with your product.

The key words in that last sentence are "best customers." Ensuring that your *best customers* remain loyal is a critical guiding principle in a customer-centric strategy. As we mentioned in chapter 1, the "80:20 rule" states that 80% of your future profits will come from just 20% of your existing customers. Following that logic, it's essential for you to know who your best customers are and to provide for their current needs while developing your portfolio to appeal to this set of "best" customers' future desires. To that end, this chapter provides strategies and best practices for effective retention and development, including up-selling and cross-selling, creating loyalty incentives, and investing in customer service.

Remember the Paradox of Customer Centricity

Before we jump into the rest of this chapter, we want to remind you of the Paradox of Customer Centricity, which we discussed in chapter 2. If an organization becomes hyperfocused on acquiring, retaining, and developing *only* its highest-value customers, it will leave itself susceptible to greater risk. Remember that while you're chasing customers with the highest CLVs, so too are your competitors. A customer-centric strategy must manage the portfolio of customers the same way financial portfolios are managed, where opportunities to make maximum financial gains are identified and fully taken advantage of, but these higher-risk bets must be weighed out and distributed across lower-risk categories of assets as well. In the same way cash and bonds provide low-risk, low-reward gains in a financial portfolio, lower-value customers serve to distribute risk and help keep the proverbial lights on.

You need to take a balanced approach to finding and retaining high-risk, high-return customers and lower-value customers. Later in this chapter, we will examine the implications this paradox has on investing in and deploying retention and development programs that are aligned with the CLV of your customers. This stage of the conversation truly gets to the heart of architecting a customer-centric strategy. We will also walk you through the strategies firms use to develop their customers.

How Firms Develop Their Customers

The meat of "customer development" can be summed up through two questions that are so well known that they're often used as punchlines:

1. Do you want fries with that?
2. Do you want to supersize it?

While these questions might have become almost comically ubiquitous, they actually aim at *cross-selling* and *up-selling*, respectively, with the goal of driving up customer value. When executed correctly, they will make already-valuable customers worth even more. And as these customers become more deeply engaged (and presumably satisfied) with your offerings, they may become stickier.

Customer development often focuses on extracting additional value from existing customers by providing more offerings that are attractive to your *best* customers. Can less-valuable customers be developed to have a better CLV? Of course! But how much should a firm focus on developing its less-valuable customers? It really depends. If you've invested to the point of diminishing returns in the development of your best customers, then it's time to turn some attention to the next lower tiers. However, you should bear in mind that when it comes to developing these less-valuable customers, you need to have the right expectations—they are unlikely to become top-tier customers no matter how much love you show them.

Cross-Selling: Do You Want Fries with That?

Getting a customer to add fries to their order is a classic example of **cross-selling**. Given that existing customers are about 50% more likely to try your other products than new customers, you should absolutely make sure these patrons know all about your full menu of offerings. Let's also pause to remember that this probability falls squarely into the "lump all our customers into one bucket" trap. There is no such thing as *the Customer*, so taking an aggregate statistic like "50% of our existing customers are more likely to purchase our other products" as gospel is a mistake. The better approach is to break this probability down by CLV tiers. At the very least, you should be considering how *often* your highest-, medium-, and lowest-value customers purchased other products. You're likely to find that the higher the customer CLV, the more likely the customer is to purchase your other offerings. For this reason, you should invest more on cross-selling or other marketing efforts that target your higher-value customers than those aimed at lower-value segments.

Online retailers have become particularly adept at cross-selling through the use of recommendation engines—think of those pop-up messages telling you, "Customers who bought [X] also purchased these six other items." Recommendation algorithms are nifty because they're unobtrusive to the shopping experience and most customers find them useful. They also don't have the same "creep factor" of other online cross-selling tactics. We've all done it—you click on a pair of trousers, only to have that same pair of khakis follow you around the internet for the next several weeks, popping up as you scroll through your social media feeds or as you try to compose an email. *"Psst! Buy me. . . . Hey, aren't you going to buy me? . . . Remember me? Want to buy me yet?"* (Is there a way to get a restraining order against apparel?)

Up-Selling: Do You Want to Supersize It?

Persuading a customer to supersize an order is **up-selling**. Another example of this classic sales tactic is when a company offers premium services, like LinkedIn Premium or Amazon Prime. Both initiatives aim to turn noncontractual customers into contractual ones by offering subscription services. In doing so, these companies now know which customers are still active, and they will have an easier time tracking and calculating the individual CLV of these customers.

A nice example of this model comes from Sarah's own household. Back in 2007, tired of the endless commercial interruptions and lack of good programming, Sarah and her husband decided to cut the cable cord the very month that Netflix started offering streaming services. But they missed being able to watch certain TV shows that Netflix didn't offer, so they soon added Hulu—a streaming service that airs episodes of just about everything on TV less than 24 hours postbroadcast—to the Rokus in their home, as well as Amazon Prime.

Hulu first launched its platform with minimal commercial interruptions. This model was preferable to the commercial-addled prime-time slog but not as good as Netflix, which had—and still has—no ads. Fast-forward to 2010, when Hulu realized it was leaving money on the table from loyal customers like the Toms, who were part of a valuable set of customers proven to have a low propensity for churn and who would be willing to pay a couple of extra dollars each month to have *no* commercials. By offering a premium upgrade that eliminated the annoyance of ads, the company made the Toms household, along with thousands of others just like it, instantly a bit more valuable (20% more valuable, to be exact). This is the driving motivation of up-selling: to extract more value from already-valuable customers by offering additional services that these customers find attractive.

Retention and Development for the Twenty-First Century

Until recently, cross-selling and up-selling boiled down to a single objective: fatten up as many faceless, nameless customers as possible. This one-size-fits-all approach is crude at best, and as discussed in the previous chapter, we can be much smarter about which tactics to use for which strategic purpose given all the data we have about individual customers. Not only are stalker khakis on the internet annoying—and as researchers from Georgia State University confirmed when they studied the cross-selling campaigns of five Fortune 1000 companies over the course of several years—they can be downright unprofitable.[47] The authors of this study summarized their findings in a *Harvard Business Review* article:

> We discovered that one in five cross-buying customers is unprofitable. That group accounts for 70% of a firm's total "customer loss"—the shortfall when the cost of goods and of marketing to a given customer exceeds the revenue realized. And the more cross-buying an unprofitable customer does, the greater the loss.[48]

A Customer-Centric Framework for Retention and Development

Data-driven technological advancements in the last half century have helped marketers fine-tune their up-selling and cross-selling tactics, such as using predictive algorithms to determine which specific products or services should be cross-sold or upsold to which individual customers. However, there are many other ways to build, sustain, and repair ongoing relationships beyond these basic tactics. Here we present a novel framework for retention and development that recognizes that different tactics are more effective depending on the individual value of the customer.

There are many retention and development (R&D) tactics out there that appear to be, to the untrained eye, substitutes for one another. The blessing and curse of R&D is that they are so deeply intertwined: a blessing because executing these seemingly intertwined tactics affords certain organizational efficiencies, and a curse because the muddied view of R&D means that organizations often fail to understand their distinctions and therefore fail to gain maximum strategic benefit.

As we think about harmonizing our R&D programs with a customer-centric strategy, we care about understanding our positioning along two dimensions:

1. *Customer Targeting: What level of value do the customers we are targeting offer?* In particular, we want to understand whether higher- or lower-value customers are the target of the program. Many companies like to group their customers into tiers labeled as precious metals, as shown in Figure 3.1: Lead is the lowest tier, and the scale then moves up through iron, silver, gold, and finally platinum, the most revered of metals—and customers. (There's a reason why platinum credit cards are reserved for only the biggest spenders.)

2. *Tactical Approach: Is offense or defense the objective of the tactic being put into play?* In playing offense, we seek growth

opportunities (developing customer value), and in playing defense, we're actively protecting the ground we've already gained (retaining already-acquired customers).

Offense tends to be associated with development, and *defense* with retention, since the former is largely opportunistic and the latter preventive. But this isn't always true; for instance, many companies (perhaps unwisely) view retention as a growth tactic. To help keep things clear, we use the more specific words *offense* and *defense* to bring sharper focus to the retention and development objectives.

We show a 2×2 framework for these two dimensions in Figure 3.2, which aligns the customer value being targeted with whether offense or defense is the main goal. In the next section, we provide the framework using one tactical example in each quadrant, but by no means are we suggesting that these are the only ones to consider. Likewise, we don't want to imply that the various example tactics always reside in one particular cell; depending how it is implemented, it could serve different objectives or even straddle multiple cells. But this should be an effective starting point to understand and appreciate the framework, and then other tactics will be easier to categorize. It is the responsibility of those in your organization investing in and implementing R&D to clearly understand where their specific programs land in this framework and whether it's the right "card to play" at any given time.

In laying out your R&D strategy in this way, you can gain clarity about whether you are over- or underinvested in a given quadrant. Ultimately, you should implement R&D tactics in a manner that appropriately aligns the goals of a program with the CLV of the customer.

What are the implications for this framework in practice? Well, remember our lead-tier customers who can't be magically alchemized into platinum customers? According to the Paradox of Customer Centricity, these customers should not be ignored, but you shouldn't overinvest in them either. For this tier of customers, loyalty programs are an effective way to squeeze out a little more value and in turn

Figure 3.1. Identify the Value of the Customer We Are Targeting

Figure 3.2. Align Customer Value with an Offense or Defense Tactic

Targeted Customers		
	High Value	Low Value
Tactical Approach — Offense	Premium Offerings	Loyalty Programs
Tactical Approach — Defense	Strategic Acct Management	Customer Service

could make a lead customer become iron (a step up, though still not even middle tier).

As this framework illustrates, strategic account managers provide defensive capabilities for high-value customers, providing white-glove assistance and support. At the other end of this dimension, customer service is positioned to provide low-touch assistance for lower-value customers. A premium offering is an offensive tactic that seeks to unlock additional profit, and it works best when targeting already-high-value customers.

On the Offense: Loyalty Programs and Premium Offerings

A classic "buy 9, get 1 free" **loyalty program**—or a more sophisticated variant—is often an effective way to squeeze a little more value out of a so-so customer, but it's not right for everyone, nor is it a panacea for every R&D problem that a company may face. (This is why loyalty programs are often perceived to underachieve.[49])

Starbucks: How Loyalty Programs Can Increase Purchase Frequency

To illustrate this point, let's look at Starbucks. As it expanded from a small business in Seattle to a worldwide powerhouse in the 1980s and 1990s, it revolutionized the coffee business. Buying a cup of coffee was no longer the simple act it had been. Starbucks became the place to meet, work, or take some "me time" while catching up with the news or social media. Indeed, Starbucks positioned itself as its customers' "third place" (after home and work) with a welcoming environment that offered creature comforts ranging from overstuffed armchairs to Wi-Fi.[50]

These types of experiences are what made Starbucks the world-class brand it is today. But growth eventually plateaued, as new coffee shops emerged that were able to replicate Starbucks's long menu of caffeine-spiked choices and welcoming ambiance. Starbucks had to adapt and change if it was going to drive the growth its shareholders demanded and counteract these new competitive threats.

With this historical backdrop in mind, at the beginning of each semester, Peter often asks his students if they think Starbucks is customer centric. Upon considering the pleasant, customer-friendly experience that many students enjoyed that very morning, most students replied yes. For a long time, Peter would then have to explain all the reasons why the traditional Starbucks model wasn't even *close* to being customer centric: You might have had a great relationship with the barista in your local Starbucks, but what happened when you went to a Starbucks down the road or in another country? It was as though someone shook the customer relationship Etch-a-Sketch and you were once again a nobody. Those other Starbucks didn't know who you were, and they certainly didn't know your value.

Fortunately, Starbucks has recently begun to show signs of shifting to a much more customer-centric model. Notably, its app now allows customers' relationships with the larger company to travel with them by way of a well-executed loyalty program. App usage also allows Starbucks to track more data on the characteristics that make up its highest-value customers—like the amount and frequency of a customer's buying habits—while also giving them extra incentives to remain loyal. In September 2015, the Starbucks app started letting customers bypass the long lines by placing and paying for their order before arriving in the store,[51] allowing them to grab and go—no waiting, no pesky exchange of cash or niceties, and no fear of being late to that first meeting or wherever else they might be headed after stopping to grab their daily caffeine fix.

These valuable morning transactions got a lot easier for a valuable segment of Starbucks's customer base . . . until they didn't. The problem was that Starbucks grossly underestimated the demand on baristas that inevitably occurred when the company launched the new service, causing huge bottlenecks at the pickup counter. Soon, walk-in customers were doing U-turns at the door when they saw crowds at the pickup counter three deep.[52] Starbucks has since added dedicated baristas for prepay orders.

While its plan had some hiccups, the moral of this story is that Starbucks had the right idea. In a noncontractual business model, it created an app that extends loyalty into a tangibly convenient service for a high-value segment of its customer base, with an added bonus of being able to easily tie actual customers to purchases and thus figure out more about who its most valuable customers are.

In early 2016, the company announced another radical change to the rules of its loyalty program that moved it squarely into the customer-centric camp. Rather than awarding loyalty points based on the *number of transactions*, Starbucks changed the program to be based on the *number of dollars* (or yen, or pounds) *spent*. This change circumvented people who tried to game the system by asking the cashier to ring up items as separate transactions to rack up those free rewards stars. This change in the rules was unpopular for a little while, but ultimately it allows Starbucks to shift to a customer-value-based program that incentivizes loyalty based on spending more.[53]

The jury is still out as to whether this loyalty program (and the overall shift toward customer centricity) will help Starbucks maintain the dominant role in the retail coffee business that it enjoyed at the turn of the century, but it says a lot about a formerly product-centric company making a bold move to create more value with its low- to mid-tier customers.

Premium Services

As good as Starbucks's loyalty program is, it's still doubtful that the program is turning iron customers into platinum ones—loyalty programs alone don't work this way. The reason why is that, for Starbucks's best customers, the incentives coming out of a loyalty program aren't actually that great. Offering an already heavy coffee consumer an incremental freebie doesn't do much for them or your business, because they would have likely bought the beverage even without the promotion. This is why, for the higher-value customers, companies need to think about what additional offerings top-tier segments need and, more importantly, are willing to pay extra for. We refer to offerings targeted at extracting additional value from high-value customers as **premium services**, though the company probably has a different name for the program—for example, Amazon Prime.

LinkedIn Premium is an example of a company doing premium offerings the right way. That said, when LinkedIn launched its premium offering, there were plenty of naysayers who complained that LinkedIn Premium was a vanity cost[54] with little actual reward. We wholeheartedly disagree with those detractors. If the program is making your company sizable returns, then who cares whether premium customers are acknowledged publicly? LinkedIn certainly doesn't care—nor should it, because its premium revenue grew 17% year over year to $162 million in late 2016,[55] just before the company was acquired by Microsoft. And in the first full quarter after the acquisition, LinkedIn made Microsoft a cool billion dollars.[56] (The actual contribution of premium revenue is no longer reported, but following the logic from when the company was reporting these figures before the acquisition, LinkedIn premium revenues made up 17%–20%[57] of the total revenue. So you do the math.)

With all the additional profit to be had, it is baffling that other social platforms such as Facebook and Twitter have yet to launch premium services. Although interestingly, in his five-hour testimony on Capitol Hill in April 2018, Mark Zuckerberg dropped a pointed hint that one day there might be a paid, premium version of Facebook. What he actually said was, "There will always be a version of Facebook that is free," which is a departure from what the company publicizes on its sign-up page (see Figure 3.3): "It's free and always will be."[58]

It's important to point out that there are right ways and wrong ways to go the extra mile for your high-value, premium customers.

Figure 3.3. Facebook's Sign-up Page

Source: Facebook screenshot, www.facebook.com/.

Remember that these customers are [of] high value for a reason: Their needs are a good match for what you're offering. In other words, they *really* like you already! Clearly, keep an eye on these customers, but don't annoy them, and certainly don't embarrass them by making too much of a fuss.

For example, Peter had a less-than-stellar experience as a high-value customer a few summers ago while flying with his family. Owing to frequent first-class trips, Peter holds top-tier status in a certain airline's frequent-flier program, but for this particular trip, he and his family were traveling in coach. Something must have triggered in the airline's database, because the next thing Peter knew, the pilot of the flight came back before takeoff to say, "We know that you usually fly first class with us, Mr. Fader. We appreciate having your whole family with you and want to make your flight as special as possible, despite being in coach." Not only did Peter find this to be an uncomfortable interaction, but when he caught the side-eye glares from nearby passengers, he was embarrassed.

So, again, while you want to make sure you pay attention to your top-tier customers, don't smother them.

Playing Defense: Customer Service and Strategic Account Management

Strategic Account Management

Moving now to the lower-left quadrant of Figure 3.2, an example of a defensive tactic that should be targeted at high-value customers is **strategic account management**—sometimes referred to as *customer success management* or other equivalent names. In reviewing a few dozen job postings for strategic account managers (SAMs)[59] on two well-known job websites, it's clear that many companies are muddling the objectives of this role, liberally mixing offensive and defensive responsibilities in an attempt to find, well, a unicorn. It's OK if this role dabbles in offensive maneuvers, but this individual shouldn't be thought of as a glorified salesperson. Rather, to be effective, SAMs must make relationship management their main concern—anticipating, preempting, and addressing the major pain points and potential sacrifices of their best customers. To this end, the most effective SAMs are trusted collaborators, problem solvers, and project managers and are able to bring innovative solutions to the table,[60] all in service of playing a high-touch, defensive strategy at the top end of the customer-value pyramid.

In the six years leading up to the recession, Autodesk Inc.—a $2 billion software company providing tools and platforms to support designers and creators—was growing impressively at approximately 15% year over year.[61] You know what happened next: The financial crisis struck in 2008, halting growth for this tech company in its tracks—that is, for every business unit except its strategic account management team, which throughout the crisis maintained its laser focus on key customers. Despite the financial climate, the SAM unit continued to grow at twice the rate of the rest of the company.[62] This unusual performance caught the attention of a business consulting firm, which decided to conduct an in-depth study of Autodesk as well as 16 SAM initiatives in other major companies. The consulting firm concluded in its 2012 report that

> Autodesk's story confirms what many leaders in the field of strategic account management have long realized: Adding value through close partnership with one's top clients brings significant rewards. At their best, high-performing SAM programs create trust and interdependence between the supplier and customer.[63]

Of course, part of the "trusted advisor" role is to point out suitable cross-selling and up-selling opportunities that may genuinely be in the client's best interests, but there's a fine line here, and the risk of creating any suspicion or skepticism in the client's eyes may more than offset the potential upside of pushing these development activities. The SAM's role is primarily (but not exclusively) a defensive one—that is, long-run value maintenance as opposed to opportunistic value creation.

Customer Service

Playing defense at the lower end of the customer-value pyramid is a different game because this tactic has to be performed at scale, which means keeping the costs down and being more reactive than proactive. Undoubtedly, one of the key elements of a successful customer retention strategy is a reliable, responsive **customer service** team. Forget about the famous actresses and pop stars that appear in companies' Super Bowl commercials—customer service reps are the real face of any company. You should invest in this team to help ensure its success, and you should take to heart the information that customer service reps can contribute about your customers' overall suggestions and concerns, which can help fine-tune your product/service offering.

Part of the customer service craft is collecting data about customer satisfaction (often in the form of Net Promoter Score®[64]) and noting any comments from customers on offerings they wish you would sell or services they'd like you to provide. This is also the team with the most crucial insight into issues related to your product, as they're getting news straight from the horse's mouth (such as when a customer is threatening to leave because of dissatisfaction). But much of this is done in the aggregate, without tying each comment back to an individual customer and then updating their CLV. This is why we frame customer service as a defensive tactic for low-tier customers. Sure, customer service is very important (particularly with the Paradox of Customer Centricity in mind), but it generally doesn't improve customer value, particularly for the top-tier customers.

Here's a bold way of looking at it. Good customer service is akin to having clean bathrooms: You have to meet certain industry standards, and you want to take pride in doing a good job of it, but it's not a way to dramatically grow the business. Yes, this is a possibly provocative statement, especially in an era in which countless companies are doubling down on **customer experience (CX) activities** with the presumption that they will not only help hold on to customers but also grow their value. We believe CX is worthwhile, but only within reason. If you are investing in CX, make sure you have a clear understanding of where it will bring returns (namely as a defensive offering for lower-tier customers) and that the big promises of CX are being formally measured (e.g., through changes in customers' CLVs before and after the CX campaign begins) so you're not unwittingly overinvesting in this new hotness.

This is why keeping Figure 3.2 top of mind is so important: Companies can't just throw R&D tactics out there and assume they will accomplish whatever goals they want to; it's critical to choose the right tool for the right purpose.

We're not ruling out the possibility that good customer service can drive some incremental sales—of course that's true. We point right back to the two key questions posed earlier in this chapter: Do you want fries with that? and Do you want to supersize it? Well-timed and well-executed cross-selling and up-selling can bring in sales that wouldn't have otherwise occurred. But it's important to recognize that these sales are often transient and opportunistic—they're usually not transformative. It's rare (but admittedly not impossible) for a particular cross-selling activity to turn an "ugly duckling" customer into a beautiful swan—or, to stay with our earlier piscine metaphor, a minnow into a whale.

Having said all that, we do see some promise in companies that are judicious in how they bring customer-level data (and analytics, such as CLV) into their customer service activities. Done right, customer service can start to take on more of an offensive/developmental role. However, realistically, for most companies that's still years away, and it's important to be well calibrated about what traditional customer service—even if well executed—can and can't do for you.

So, to summarize, we see customer service as a critical must-have for companies, but primarily for defensive purposes. It is easy to over-invest in it, and the return on investment on those excessive efforts should be watched closely as they are likely quite limited. But at the same time, we encourage firms to run limited—and carefully measured—experiments to start to learn how to achieve growth through customer service as well.

Nuances of Offensive and Defensive R&D Play

The tactics we've used as examples in this chapter are by no means meant to be taken as an exhaustive list of every possible R&D tactic. Indeed, there are many more—and firms seem to be inventing new ones (or at least relabeling old ones) every day. We use these examples because they're common in business and consumer contexts, which makes them relatable. Our real objective for you is to think about tuning your R&D implementation to

- whether the objective is offense or defense, and
- being intentional about where on the customer-value pyramid you are targeting the tactic.

Another point we want to make, which came up during the SAM and customer service discussions, is that the tactics we describe may not sit perfectly in one of the Figure 3.2 quadrants, but may spill into neighboring quadrants. As another such example, loyalty programs may also play a defensive role, because the points and extra goodies that customers receive may be keeping them as customers, even if they're having some doubts. This kind of customer lock-in isn't a source of enhanced value per se, but it can be a great way to play defense.[65]

We acknowledge that these kinds of spillovers are a limit of the black-and-white nature of a 2×2 framework. In reality there is a more fine-grained spectrum for each dimension, and thus there is room for additional "shades of gray" tactics that may allow firms to achieve an even better balance in allocating R&D resources to different customers. But in an era where these R&D activities tend to be a disorganized jumble of shotgun tactics, it's important to start simple and create some initial alignment (and accountability) before going too far.

Chapter Summary

- The Paradox of Customer Centricity states that the more you obsess over acquiring the best customers, the more you need

to retain and develop some lower-value customers to help
balance out your business.

- Cross-selling ("Do you want fries with that?") and up-selling
  ("Do you want to supersize it?") are traditional customer-
  development approaches designed to drive up customer value.
- A more customer-centric approach of retaining and
  developing customers means using customer value to
  determine when a firm should use an offensive strategy
  (loyalty programs and premium offerings) or defensive
  strategy (customer service and strategic account management).

Chapter 4

CRM's Place in Creating
a Value-Based Strategy

Customer relationship management (CRM) is essential to any modern business strategy that depends on managing complex interactions with customers—which is to say, pretty much all of them. In the view of major CRM providers, a well-executed CRM system is a technological solution that serves as the nerve center of the business, enabling growth and profitability by helping to make sense of massive amounts of customer data from multiple streams, such as sales, marketing, customer service, and social media.[66]

Paul Greenberg, author of *CRM at the Speed of Light*, foresaw decades ago that CRM would eventually connect all business relationships—though he laments to this day that CRM hasn't advanced beyond a technology platform into an organizational linchpin that incorporates more holistic views, integrating strategy, philosophy, and corporate culture.[67] Nevertheless, from the foresight of Greenberg to the astronomical success of Salesforce, the theory behind CRM sounds fabulous. But does a proper CRM system *really* matter all that much to the bottom line?

In a word, yes. Look no further than the popularity of Ring video doorbells or Nest "learning" thermostats to understand the reasons that now, more than ever, CRM is incredibly relevant. The internet revolution is only just getting warmed up, and it will continue to transform the way customers—both individuals and enterprises—purchase and use goods and services.

Many organizations have been caught off guard by the rapid pace at which the internet has evolved, leaving those that struggle with adjusting to these modern ways in the virtual dust. Web 1.0 gave customers access to predominantly static information, like the Wikipedia-type websites that served as electronic classifieds and online shopping carts that digitized paper-catalog versions produced by the very same companies. Then Web 2.0 came along, transforming the internet experience by, among many other things, bringing hyper-interactivity to social platforms, thereby putting users—not businesses—at the center of web content creation. Currently, we are on the verge of Web 3.0 being fully realized, where the internet will become increasingly shaped by machine learning, artificial intelligence (AI), and the preference algorithms that companies such as Amazon and Netflix introduced in earlier incarnations and continue to perfect. Web 3.0 will be a semantic, artificially intelligent, and deeply personalized web that anticipates the future desires, emotional responses, and predictive behaviors of customers through analysis of everything people do online—and everything people's *things* do, including their connected homes, wearable devices, AI personal assistants, smart cars, and smart washing machines. In this emerging reality, *everything* will be connected via the Internet of Things (IoT).[68]

Imagine the possibilities for businesses once IOT is fully realized: all the data about a single customer perpetually generated and sent back to companies, all day every day. Imagine how differently customers will make purchases: Will routine purchasing decisions such as the weekly grocery list and monthly prescription reorders be handed off to the IOT? Will customers relinquish even more purchasing control for some of the larger decisions, enabling their refrigerator or mobile phone to decide that it's time to be replaced and order the upgraded version of itself on the customer's behalf? More than likely, yes.

Ten years ago, this all would have sounded a bit far-fetched, but no longer. Companies must embrace the explosion of customer information in this omni-channel reality, which is already coalescing.

Now think about the implications for the firms that produce and distribute these goods and services, especially those that aim to be customer centric as we define it here. The ability to "celebrate heterogeneity" and act on it in real time will become more promising (if not more essential) than ever before. All of the data structures and related marketing tactics discussed throughout this book will seem positively quaint in a few years.

To that end, with data storage costs being pennies on the dollar, there has been a shift in mindset and less fear of collecting massive sets of data even before a firm knows what it's going to do with it. Firms no longer feel as though they have to be neat about data collection and have recently shifted from the selective, structured approach of a database to a "data lake," where the goal is to collect as much raw, unstructured data as possible, opting to extract and actually make sense of the data later on during analysis.[69]

This vision is, of course, a blessing and a curse. Customer centricity, with its emphasis on long-run value creation over short-run transactional gains, needs to be executed carefully and deliberately—not opportunistically. Accordingly, you must understand the barebones requirements that CRM must provide in order to build a future-proofed, customer-value-based strategy. Stated differently, you need to know which data elements are *truly important* versus merely "nice to know." Peter touched on some of these issues in his earlier book on customer centricity, but here we take a deeper dive—getting specific about which data elements are most mission critical, first to calculate CLV properly and then to fully leverage CRM to create and measure enhanced value for the strategically important customers (and by extension, the customer base as a whole).

Integrating CLV into CRM

If you're developing a customer-value-based strategy, you must first understand the basics of calculating customer value before you can assess whether your CRM system provides the insights needed to support a customer-centric strategy, remembering to avoid the common mistakes we covered in chapter 1. While database market-ing is often considered outdated these days, many of its principles remain applicable to basic customer value calculations.[70]

We focus here on the data and customer analytics that your CRM must provide in order to support your comprehension of customer value. Ultimately, you need your CRM to help predict the factors that calculate the CLV of your existing customers so that you can take the appropriate approaches to R&D, as described in chapter 3. Additionally, your CRM is the key to helping proactively identify who your highest-value *future* customers are likely to be, based on the data gathered on existing high-value customers.

Let's break this down further, so you can ensure your CRM is collecting these key pieces of information correctly in order to ulti-mately calculate CLV the right way.

Make sure customers are consistently defined and uniquely identified in the CRM system.

We have stated many times that there is no such thing as *the Customer*, but for CRM reporting calculations it is important for you to have a clear understanding and consensus on the definition of "customer" in your organization. For example, are they the individual decision makers, buyers, or users? Defining who your customer is in the same way across your organization is important as you build out and track information in your CRM *about* these customers.

In this regard, it's fine—actually, it's better—to track customers at the more granular level (e.g., at the user level) and then connect customers together at the enterprise level. Be aware that even though technology makes it easier than ever to collect the myriad touchpoints we have with customers—like phone numbers, credit card transac-tions, mobile app hits, loyalty program membership, browser cookies, and other device IDs—it's really important that all these data are consolidated and assigned to the original owner so that any given customer isn't double-counted.

Make it a burning priority to link as many purchases (and other activities) as possible to specific customers.

Many of the aforementioned tracking technologies are seen as pure costs, but they really are foundationally critical to launching customer centricity. To this end, it is important for organizations to make it easy and desirable for customers to willingly self-identify every time they interact with you if it's not possible to identify who these customers are via automated means. You cannot build a customer-centric strategy if your customers remain anonymous to you. More and more companies are offering incentives to make purchases through their apps or have stopped taking cash altogether, meaning they are able to identify and track every purchase back to a specific customer. Certainly, there are costs and operational drivers behind these maneuvers, but they also align with the move toward customer-centric tracking. But here's the catch: Try to avoid offering discounts to unmask customer identities, because this tends to be bait to attract and keep low-value customers.

Be very careful about how you account for customer costs.

Obviously, any costs that can be directly tied to each specific customer should be accounted for, but it's debatable whether broad overhead costs—like those associated with a big ad campaign—should be amortized across the customer base. How you choose to attribute the returns on those costs might depend on whether the campaign was directly customer-facing (like for CX) or not (like for a TV ad campaign). In addition, if you are investing in a large advertising campaign to attract new customers, be sure that you are tracking those customers acquired by this effort.

Another example that might be unclear with respect to cost is how product returns are handled. For example, do you (a) pretend the original purchase never happened; (b) assume it did happen, but give it zero monetary value (or maybe lower, due to processing costs);

or (c) count both touchpoints (purchase and return) as "transactions" since there was engagement for both? It's hard to say what the right answer is, but what is important is that you're consistent in your accounting for costs associated with returns.

Bottom line: It's essential for marketing and accounting to have some deep discussions about these issues to get mutual buy-in and to revisit these issues frequently.

Think carefully about whether nonpurchase activities are "baked in" to the CLV model directly or used just for profiling/targeting purposes afterward.

When contemplating the incorporation of nonfinancial activities into your CLV calculation, most times we would caution against doing this directly within the CLV formula. But, we would also recommend that capturing these types of activities outside CLV may still be relevant. Think about the additional value a company may want to assign to the endorsement from an internet celebrity or the volunteer hours of a supporting nonprofit member, like National Public Radio. Ask yourself: Does this nonfinancial activity really help make better long-run predictions about value (and do you know how to include it in the CLV model), or is this activity just "nice to know"?

Collaborate with the finance and accounting folks to choose the most appropriate discount factor(s).

It's important to carefully quantify the "riskiness" of your customer base, recognizing that—just like everything else we know to be true about our customers—the risk profile of the customer base is also heterogeneous. CLV is calculated using the average revenue of a certain customer for a certain number of periods into the future. While potentially useful, predicting future revenue is always risky. In that sense, revenue received in the future is *less valuable* than if it is received today, which is why CLV calculations include a discount rate. Discount rates are based on the time value concept of money—the premise that a dollar today is worth more than a dollar tomorrow. Accordingly, discount rates allow us to calculate the present value of predicted future revenue, given risk.

Using a discount rate is a useful way to account for risk, and though it's unusual, it's perfectly acceptable to use different discount rates for different subgroups of customers to account for the varying level of risk found in your customer base. There are no hard-and-fast rules for how to calculate the discount rate, and it will likely depend on your company. Accordingly, it is also extremely important that discount rates are revisited frequently with your finance team.

Given that so much of expected customer value lives in the future—where there are risks of the market changing, of new competition, of a disruptive technology, or of unanticipated internal business turmoil—the risk factored into the discount rate is meant to account for anything that could impact future profitability.

Electronic Arts (EA): A Study in CRM and Lifetime Value

There are many important questions you need to ask when evaluating your CRM:

- Does my CRM provide an accurate picture of the heterogeneous landscape of my current and future customer base with respect to value and risk?
- Does my CRM tell me who my most valuable customers are in the first place? If so, is the information tracked about customers useful in making predictions on how to maximize customer value?
- Does my CRM provide meaningful insight into my existing high-value customers, allowing me to make targeted investments into efforts that find, acquire, retain, and develop *other* high-value customers?

We first talked about EA's incredible turnaround in the introduction.[71] This is a company that has worked fastidiously over the past decade to build capabilities that provide a "yes" to each of these questions— and in doing so has increased stock values several times over.

EA predates the internet by about a decade. Naturally, not being digitally native has brought its own set of challenges, but this has also helped the company in some surprising ways. Certainly, the analysts at EA would like their insights to be taken at face value and adopted quickly. But more often than not, when new data are presented to decision makers, things slow down a bit as the data go through intense questioning and scrutiny (a translation process that Ben Tisdale believes is a vestige of the company's predigital culture), and this step has become vital in how information is put into action at EA. By not taking every metric at face value and instead taking time to understand which data are worthwhile and deserve attention, the older, arguably more data-wary culture is actually supporting the success of modern analytical approaches by demanding further rigor.

The CLV[72] of individual players is now a universally accepted data point at EA, and one that is cut multiple ways to build a holistic picture about players—which is in service of its "Player First" mission. Put into practice, when players' CLVs increase, this means these players are probably having a good time and will prompt analysts to try to figure out why. (And of course, the converse is true as well.) In turn, information about what players are doing in the game and where they are most (and least) engaged is then sent back to the game studios to help inform future game design.

CRM across Companies

So far, our discussion of CRM's place in calculating customer value has been fairly straightforward. However, some firms face a high degree of complexity in deciding when to count a customer as being acquired, when to consider them retained, and when to write them off as lost, which can complicate the role of CRM. Is a customer

Figure 4.1. The Gap.com Homepage

Source: "Gap.com," Shop Gap, www.gap.com/, accessed October 3, 2018.

gained upon becoming a customer to your parent company, or is it when they become a customer of your individual brand (or a family of brands in a product vertical)?

For example, does parent company Gap Inc. know the CLV of a customer who shops at more than one of its brands? When customers visit gap.com (or athleta.com, oldnavy.com, or bananarepublic.com), they can browse and purchase from any other Gap Inc. brand, as shown in Figure 4.1. In theory, the company should be able to track purchases across multiple brands back to a single customer. Indeed, Gap Inc.'s CEO Art Peck confirmed in an April 2018 *Mad Money* interview that, for two years prior, the company had invested heavily in its big data and customer analytics capabilities. He credits this strategic shift to customer centricity for the improvement in share prices from $18 in May 2016 to $29 just two years later:

> We know a lot about our customers. We can see their lifetime value. We know who our most valuable customer is. Structurally, because we have multiple brands and multi-channels, we've got something not a lot of other apparel companies have. If you look at the difference between a customer who's casually engaged and one who is really deeply engaged in our brands across channels, it's at least 10 times the value of that [first] customer.[73]

Figure 4.2. Cox Enterprises Companies: Brands

Cox Communications
Cox Automotive
Autotrader®
Clutch Technologies
Dealer.com®
Dealertrack®
Kelley Blue Book®
Manheim®
NextGear Capital®
VinSolutions®
vAuto®
Xtime
Cox Media Group
14 television stations
1 local cable channel
4 daily newspapers
60+ radio stations
80 digital sites
Local and regional advertising services

Source: Cox Enterprises Businesses, "How We're Different," https://www.coxenterprises.com/about-us/businesses, accessed 08/24/2018.

Cox Enterprises—a massive conglomerate of media, automotive, and financial service companies—is another example; just look at Figure 4.2 to see its impressive portfolio of brands. Cox is one of the largest privately held companies in the United States[74] and another great example of the conundrum of how and when to track customers in a firm with a complex, sometimes unrelated set of business offerings.

From the perspective of tracking customers, companies like Cox should track acquisition at the point the customer first becomes a customer of *any* of its business units—and when an existing customer signs up for an offering from a different business unit within the company, they should not be counted as a new customer. When it comes to the CLV of a single customer across multiple business units, the only way these large conglomerates can track the big picture is by either (1) having an enterprise CRM system that tracks, shares, and rolls up information about customer interactions across the entire business or (2) feeding customer data from each individual business unit's respective CRM into a master system so that information about customer value can be analyzed holistically.

But the reality is that conglomerates like Gap Inc. and Cox Enterprises tend to acquire brands by purchasing already-established companies, which makes it unlikely that the acquired company's CRM can be easily integrated with its new parent company. The leadership would have to make a concerted effort to unify the tracking of customer interactions across all the brands, just as Gap Inc. has accomplished. But after a typical acquisition, it can take years before all the business units are on a single, integrated system; if that's the case, and if customer centricity is the strategic goal, then the firm will need to figure out how to collect data about its customers to inform strategy.

Maybe you're not grappling with the aftermath of a complicated merger and acquisition, but ask yourself this: When it comes to how you think about customer value, does your firm have ironclad silos that are rigidly aligned with product offerings that aren't integrating information about customers across silos?

When thinking of companies that fall into this category, traditional banks and financial service companies come to mind. What happens when an existing checking and savings account customer tries to sign up for a mortgage or an IRA? Often, the experience from the customer's perspective is that they're treated like a nobody because the mortgage department has absolutely no awareness of the customer beyond the product line that the specific department services. In the customer-centric world, not recognizing who the high-value customers are—regardless of which products they have bought—is a cardinal sin.

The Limits of CRM

So, here's the catch. You might have heard the adage, When you have a hammer, everything looks like a nail. Just because a CRM system is tracking vast information about your customers doesn't mean it is realistically equipped to provide all the insights required to support a customer-centric strategy. It is *your* responsibility to develop the scorecard and key performance indicators necessary to measure the degree to which you're successfully developing your firm's customer value. There will likely be both tiny and yawning gaps in the data you'll need that your CRM both can and cannot provide. Do not take these shortfalls sitting down! It is the responsibility of the business executives formulating the strategy to challenge their CRM providers to close these gaps. (They like having your business, which means they'll go out of their way to deliver.)

Also remember that rolling out a CRM system on Monday doesn't mean that you'll have all the answers by Tuesday. A successful customer-centric strategy only works in the first place if it's closely aligned with your CRM solution. Is your firm actively ensuring this alignment? If not, don't be surprised when the CRM system you've spent five or more figures to implement falls short. Also, don't take the data analysis from your CRM on blind faith. You still have a responsibility to test any assertions implied by the data. For example, how accurate are the current predictions made by your CRM about CLV, retention rates, or customer acquisition for a particular customer segment? If the comparison is way off, it's time to get the CRM vendor on the phone and figure out why.

Speaking of which, how is your *relationship* with your CRM vendor? (Serious question and pardon the intentional pun!) Do they fully understand the goals of your plan to develop a customer-centric strategy? Are they clear about your expectations and what that means in terms of supporting your needs? If not, then you need a plan that addresses these gaps in practical terms, or even the best-intended plans to achieve transformation through heightened data analysis will wither on the vine. Gene Marks addressed exactly these limitations in his *Forbes* article "11 Terrible CRM Systems for Your Company." Marks concluded that all 11 systems he looked at weren't what was terrible; rather, the organizations themselves failed to establish supporting processes for the CRM initiatives. He explains that issues arise for CRM when leadership takes a passive role in supporting CRM and fails to demand the reports needed to inform their own strategic initiatives.[75] (We discuss these issues in more detail in chapter 6.)

Developing Your CRM to Support a Customer-Centric Strategy

Sarah has spent the majority of her 20-plus-years career in technology working with global companies to develop and integrate CRM, IT service management, and enterprise-relationship-planning systems. She's learned the hard way that for these tools to deliver on their transformational promises, they must

- align with and support the organization's overall strategy; and
- light the path for process and business improvement initiatives by providing evidence (in the way of data) that the organization is moving in the right direction, or that a course correction is warranted.

Where she begins with large-scale projects like these is to work with stakeholders to define the critical success factors (CSFs) of the business and identify four or five key performance indicators (KPIs) for each CSF. Next, a target is set for each KPI, and if performance is below target, a warning bell sounds, making managers aware that a CSF may be at risk. Rolling up KPI data to the CSF level also provides a tidy way of looking at the health of business goals, and this approach provides a practical way for staff and leadership to communicate about how the business is measuring success.

It's easy to see how this practical exercise can serve as the basis for executive dashboards in your CRM. It provides a way to communicate requirements about the insights management and staff need back to the technologists tasked with integrating the system. If your CRM approach doesn't corral, organize, and tie the metrics back to the strategic goals of the organization in this way, prepare yourself to be underwhelmed with the performance of your CRM.

Speaking of reporting dashboards, out of the box you'll find that a lot of CRM reports are redundant or downright useless. Organizations have a further responsibility to own the reports that they depend on and to build their own in-house business intelligence capability. In many cases, we've seen higher degrees of sophistication when companies take the raw data from their CRM and produce their own reports.

In order to develop your CRM to support a customer-centric strategy, start by thinking about the central tactics of customer centricity—acquisition, retention, and development—and then ensure that everything necessary to measure CLV is being tracked.

Remember that analyzing these data at the highest aggregated level won't provide as much insight as doing customer-segment comparisons. Another key step is to keep your eye on how various rates are changing over time—and, in particular, that the rates are moving in the right direction per the targets you set for your KPIs. Last but not least, take to heart what we cautioned about in earlier chapters about the pitfalls of traditional approaches to segmentation and customer personas.

Chapter Summary

- An effective CRM system is integral to any modern business strategy that depends on managing complex interactions with customers throughout customers' lifetimes.
- However, CRM has its limits, as there will always be gaps in data within the system. Leaders within your organization have a responsibility to challenge CRM providers to close these gaps.

- Companies can integrate CLV into CRM by (1) making sure customers are consistently defined and uniquely identified in the CRM system, (2) prioritizing linking as many purchases/ activities as possible to specific customers, (3) being judicious about how they account for customer costs, (4) deciding whether nonpurchase activities are "baked in" to the CLV model up front, and (5) working with the finance and accounting teams to choose appropriate discount factor(s).
- A CRM can support your organization's overall customer-centric strategy by providing evidence—through data—of whether the company is moving in a good direction or whether it needs to retool its approach.

Chapter 5

The Role of Customer Centricity in Corporate Valuation

I n our experience, we have found that customer centricity can be introduced through several different parts of the organization. Most often it is the marketing department that first recognizes and pushes ahead with this kind of strategy, but that's not always the case. As an intriguing alternative, we have seen several successful cases in which the finance department got the ball rolling—and created greater buy-in across the organization than the marketers could achieve.

This chapter will provide you with a primer on traditional firm valuation methods, the concepts of brand equity and customer equity, and advice on how to recognize when growth periods are behind you. We will also discuss some recent research regarding Wayfair and Blue Apron's addiction to acquisition, delving into why this unhealthy dependence doesn't bode well for either company's valuation.

Methods of Firm Valuation

Traditional approaches to measuring a firm's value tell only a portion of the story.[76] Sure, these approaches do a good job accounting for the equity derived from financial and operational assets. But from a conventional viewpoint, any notion of what customers contribute to the balance sheet in terms of brand equity and customer value is missing entirely from these approaches. If you look at the entries in the "C" section of the index of most books on corporate valuation—such as best-selling *Valuation* by our Wharton colleague David

Figure 5.1. Conventional Equities in Market Valuation

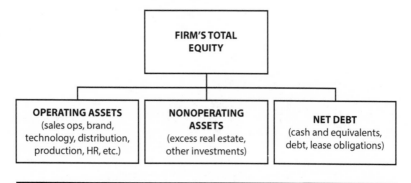

Wessels and coauthors[77] or Aswath Damodaran's *Little Book of Valuation*[78]—there is no substantive discussion about customers and the value they contribute.

For anyone not fluent in business finance, let's run through a quick overview of some key terminology. **Net income** refers to total revenue minus expenses and taxes (you'll often see *net income* and *cashflow* used interchangeably with *gross profit*). Obviously, a healthy net income means a company is profitable, which is a good indication that it's doing well when measured across two specific dimensions: revenue and expenses.

Market valuation, on the other hand, takes a wider view than profitability alone by looking at what *potential* value is added to the business by investing in conventional assets like technology, operational equipment, and staff, as shown in Figure 5.1. This approach makes sense because, for example, if a food manufacturer recently upgraded its production lines to be more efficient and require less overhead to produce sellable goods, then it's likely that investors will view this spend favorably, as it improves the firm's potential profitability. The same goes for a technology investment deemed to improve staff productivity.

Firms invest an estimated 8% of GDP in the marketing activities associated with acquiring, retaining, and developing customers.[79] Executives may not say it explicitly to their investors, but by committing this level of spend, they clearly see tremendous value associated with their customers. (On the flip side, with so much being spent on tactics related to acquiring and retaining customers, isn't it odd that investors don't demand more insight into the return on such investments? Very odd, indeed!)

Brand Equity

Thankfully, perspectives are beginning to shift. In recent years, there has been growing acceptance that an emerging class of corporate assets—classified as **brand equity (BE)**—exists and plays an important role in market valuation, either by providing a boost (in the case of a strong brand that customers *believe in*) or by having the opposite effect (if customers have negative associations with a brand).

After cofounding Apple, a young Steve Jobs knew he could differentiate the user experience by creating an emotional connection to his brand. "The chance to make a memory is the essence of brand marketing," he famously said at the time. Jobs was wildly successful in reaching this goal, making technology choice a deeply personal—almost religious—decision, despite there not being many functional differences between an iPhone and, say, a Samsung Galaxy (hence why these companies are constantly suing each other over intellectual property infringements[80]).

Consider what happens when an awful customer experience becomes widely known, like in the case of United Airlines. In early 2017, an elderly customer's face was bashed in during a struggle in which he was literally dragged off a plane at the request of airline staff. The entire event was caught on video by horrified onlookers and quickly went viral. In reality, overzealous airport security officers—not United's staff—assaulted the passenger, yet United's brand reputation suffered in the aftermath, including taking an $800 million hit to its value[81] after the upsetting event.

While virtually all marketing experts agree that the value of a brand plays an important part in overall market valuation, the science around measuring a brand's formal financial value is far from exact. The problem with landing on a specific number is that the effects of the brand persist throughout the customer life cycle.

For example, a strong brand with better overall awareness than its competitors and a good reputation may find it cheaper to acquire new customers who are willing to pay more for its product or service than they would elsewhere. The strength of that same brand could also boost loyalty with existing customers, which becomes particularly important (and quite valuable) when there's a competitive threat. (Doesn't this sound a lot like our earlier discussion about *customer goodness*? This is no coincidence; more to come on this important connection.)

Perhaps this has happened to you: You have a preferred brand in a particular category, but a competing brand releases an objectively better product offering. However, you're willing to ride things out and wait until a similar product (even if it's still a bit inferior) is offered by *your* brand. When a brand's reputation is strong enough, it can make for stickier customers, even when a customer's chosen brand might not have, say, the most feature-rich offering at the time. Accordingly, brand plays an important role in company equity.

There are countless measurement schemes that attempt to calculate brand equity,[82] though there is also understandable debate over whether calculating an exact dollar value is realistic. Probably the best-known brand-valuation exercise is carried out by the Interbrand agency. As reported in its 2017 ranking of the top 100 brands,[83] Apple and Google, respectively, were deemed the most and second most valuable brands in the world, as shown in Figure 5.2. These rankings should come as no surprise, but was Apple's brand worth *exactly* $184,154 million and Google's brand worth *exactly* $141,703 million at the *exact* time of this report? Probably not. If it seems dubious to you that brand value can be calculated with six significant digits of precision, then you're in the same skeptical camp that we are—and we suspect that virtually every CFO in the world would agree.

We're not saying that the Apple brand isn't worth *about* $200 billion; rather, we're saying that the ability to come up with a more precise estimate is problematic and not very trustworthy.

Figure 5.2. Interbrand's Best Global Brands 2017 Rankings

Rank	Brand	Brand Value
1	Apple	$184,154 m
2	Google	$141,703 m
3	Microsoft	$79,999 m
4	CocaCola	$69,733 m
5	Amazon	$64,796 m
6	Samsung	$56,249 m
7	Toyota	$50,291 m
8	Facebook	$48,188 m
9	Mercedes	$47,829 m
10	IBM	$46,829 m

Source: "Best Brands," Interbrand, December 2017, interbrand.com/best-brands/best-global-brands /2017/ranking/.

What you should take away from this discussion is that investment in your company's brand is vitally important, but we cannot realistically measure the value of a brand per se, nor can we direct brand-related spending to help drive or inform the implementation of specific customer-centric strategies and tactics (such as acquisition, retention, and development).

Customer Equity

A far more quantifiable measurement of the value derived from your customer base is **customer equity (CE)**, which is defined as the sum of all present (and ideally, *future*) customer CLVs. With that in mind, we'd like to circle back to our previously mentioned befuddlement regarding the fact that investors aren't demanding to see more information about the value of a firm's customer base, given the resources directed to acquiring customers. With so much spent on the brand and customers in general, investors certainly deserve to understand whether there is a justifiable return on their investment, and company leadership have a fiduciary responsibility to provide these data.

Interestingly, there has been a recent groundswell of investors, accountants, and economists who all seem to agree that customer equity–based measurements can no longer be ignored when determining the book value of a firm.[84] Accountants and economists alike have noticed that the models they've been using to measure "rational" markets are missing a customer value component. Through careful analysis, they've found that customers are sticking around longer than they rationally should. Experts agree that this trend points to a need to account for the effects customers have on firm value.

These other fields refer to this phenomenon as *customer franchise* or *customer capital*. Whether you use the term *customer equity* or a different term, the important point is that you don't have to take customer equity as gospel only from marketing experts anymore. There is now widespread agreement and corroboration from experts across multiple fields that the value customers bring to the balance sheet is real, that it should be measured, and, gosh darn it, that it should be reported to (and demanded by) investors!

In other words, a firm's total equity is measured by the factors shown in Figure 5.3.

Figure 5.3. Adding Customers into the Firm Valuation Equation

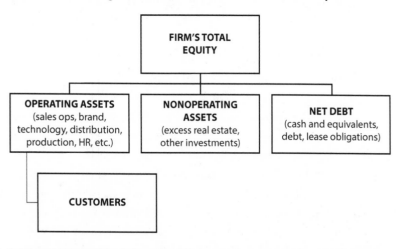

The BE versus CE Debate

There are two camps when it comes to reconciling which is more important: BE or CE. Peter described this tension in his last book but left the reader with the impression that this is purely an either/or question, with one right answer and one wrong answer (which may differ from one context to another). Our more refined view today is that the two equities overlap, as shown in Figure 5.4.

Proponents of BE argue that the value of the brand manifests itself in many ways above and beyond additional purchases. For example, a strong brand makes it easier to hire star employees (and do so more inexpensively), which will help the company communicate with the general public more effectively and could translate into financial and nonfinancial rewards when dealing with government officials (e.g., securing tax advantages). These benefits are undeniable.

In contrast, those advocating for CE take the long view: They believe that most of the advantages arising from a strong brand (including all those just noted) may not lead to more purchases tomorrow, but they will eventually manifest through CE—in better customers acquired more efficiently, in maintaining longer relationships, and in driving more value while alive. So while we acknowledge that there is a portion of the above Venn diagram where BE

Figure 5.4. A Venn Diagram of BE and CE

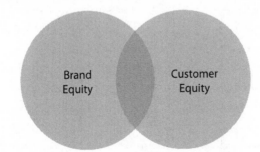

Brand
Equity

Customer
Equity

Figure 5.5. A Venn Diagram Showing BE as a CE Component

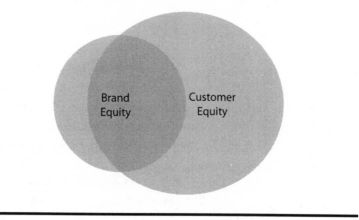

stands alone, our view is that the majority of BE can arise from (and be measured through) CLV, and thus can be attributed as a component under CE, as shown in Figure 5.5.

This is not in any way a knock against the power of the brand or its ability to create lasting value. On the contrary, we see branding as a powerful component of an effective customer-centric strategy—it's just hard to measure on its own. It is deeply intertwined with the other, more tangible aspects of customer centricity (e.g., acquisition, retention, development) and makes them easier to achieve and more impactful than they would be without a strong brand attached to them.

Put another way, we see branding as the *lubrication for the customer centricity engine*. All the different parts work better on their own and avoid friction when they interface with each other. A strong brand enhances the effectiveness and efficiency of the creation of customer goodness, often in ways that are not achievable through other tactics. This is (literally) an invaluable role—meaning that its system-wide value is very high, but the ability to formally quantify it is extremely limited.

With this in mind, we will now move on from our discussion of branding and BE, but you should keep it in mind as we turn our discussion back to the more quantifiable elements of a customer-centric strategy, starting—as always—with customer acquisition.

The Startling Effects of Acquisition Addiction on Corporate Valuation

We've said it before and we'll say it again: Smart acquisition is the main driver for customer centricity. Retention and development both factor in for sure, but if you don't have the right customers in the first place, your customer-centric strategy will never achieve the profit potential for which you strive. The problem is that this focus on acquisition can lead to an unhealthy obsession.

For the most part, Wall Street judges the worth of firms in two ways: top-line growth and bottom-line growth. A firm's top line is the gross revenue generated from sales, and the bottom line is the net income, or profitability, of the firm (in other words, what's left in the coffers after all expenses are deducted from the top-line sales). A note from Investopedia on the subject:

> Both these figures are useful in determining the financial strength of a company, but they are not interchangeable. Bottom line describes how efficient a company is with its spending and operating costs and how effectively it has been controlling total costs. Top line, on the other hand, only indicates how effective a company is at generating sales and does not take into consideration operating efficiencies which could have a dramatic impact on the bottom line.[85]

As companies mature, their strategies should shift from growing the top line through more sales and more customers to focusing on the care and feeding of the bottom line—which, to succeed, requires driving more investment toward retaining and developing existing high-value customers.

Firms are notoriously bad at making this transition. Psychologically, the growth phase of a company marks the rah-rah heydays

Figure 5.6. Business Maturity over Time

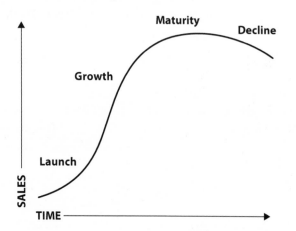

Source: Marshall Fisher, Vishal Gaur, and Herb Kleinberger, "Curing the Addiction to Growth," Harvard Business Review, January 1, 2017, hbr.org/2017/01/curing-the-addiction-to-growth.

where corporate success is measured in acquiring lots of new customers. When success is achieved, this elated feeling moves virally from the boardroom to the huddle spaces in cubicle farms. This is a time when most of the staff is being hired and executives' careers are being forged; the culture and values of the company are being cast from a narrative that corporate success comes from growing the top line.

And because the company has experienced growth in only one way thus far—through customer acquisition—executives at the helm hold fast to this strategy, driving their teams to overwhelmingly seek out opportunities that yield yet more growth through acquisition long after the glorious growth phase has set behind the peak of the classic S-curve that tracks a company's development trajectory—or indeed, the maturity of the marketplace, as depicted in Figure 5.6.

This represents a narrow-sightedness that is rooted in human nature and is perpetuated by the values that underpin corporate cultures that are—not to put too fine a point on it—often myopic and difficult to change.

Why does it matter that a company is deriving the majority of its revenue from purchases made by new customers if sales targets are being met? A number of recent marketing research studies have been taking a close look at this question and have found some troubling results that don't bode well for the long-term viability of firms that are shown to have an unhealthy dependency on customer acquisition. Indeed, one such study was coauthored by Peter and Professor Dan McCarthy of Emory University. Using publicly disclosed customer data, Peter and Dan were able to determine a **customer-based corporate valuation (CBCV)** for two noncontractual online retailers, Overstock and Wayfair. While the CBCV analysis for Overstock yielded a valuation estimate within 10% of its market valuation at the time of the analysis, the study found that Wayfair loses about $10 on every customer it acquires, so its stock is overvalued by as much as 84%[86]—a finding that sent shockwaves through the stock market hours after the first draft of the study was initially released.[87]

Professor McCarthy released a related study in mid-2017 about the initial public offering (IPO) filing for meal-kit provider Blue Apron,[88] another company that was called out for its unhealthy addiction to customer acquisition. Before the IPO (and before McCarthy's analysis), Blue Apron seemed to many to be a solid-enough investment opportunity. In five short years, the company had grown to one million customers and $790 million.[89] As McCarthy's analysis revealed, the problem was that most of those customers weren't sticking around for very long. In his own words about these findings:

> Blue Apron doesn't retain customers for very long, and the cost to acquire customers has been on the rise lately. These are important ingredients to the overall customer-based corporate valuation recipe.[90]

McCarthy found that Blue Apron's initial projected share price of about $15 was significantly overvalued given its unsatisfactory customer churn. He calculated that, at best, the price should be

Figure 5.7. New York Stock Exchange Historical Market Summary, 2017–2018: Blue Apron Holdings Inc.

Source: "Market Summary > Blue Apron Holding Inc.," Google search result for stock ticker APRN on March 6, 2018. Results are a feed from Google Finance, Yahoo Finance, and MSN Money.

barely half that amount—again, *at best*. As these CBCV calculations predicted, and as shown in Figure 5.7, the bottom has fallen out of Blue Apron's share price since its IPO, dropping well below $3 per share.

The Blue Apron IPO has become a cautionary tale for how companies are valued on Wall Street. The health of any business is measured in part by looking at both the number of new customers it acquires and at what cost as well as what percentage of value is being derived period after period from those newly acquired customers. If a business is attracting hordes of customers whose lifetime values do not exceed the cost to acquire them, it has a problem.

Peter and Dan are very serious about moving CBCV into everyday business practice: In May 2018 they incorporated Theta Equity Partners[91] to make these kinds of bottom-up valuation analyses available to a broad range of investors. Their hope, beyond the success of this one corporate entity, is to get more investors to drive their investment decisions based, in part, on the value of a firm's customer assets—and to know when it's the right time to take their foot off the customer-acquisition accelerator.

Recognizing When the Growth Phase Is Behind You

Now that we have provided you with some customer acquisition strategies and best practices, we want to spend a little time discussing when acquisition should *not* be your company's focus.

Customer acquisition, even if profitable, is finite. There are always people within any population who will not adopt a company's products or services, and the faster the population adopts the innovation you're selling, the faster the acquisition numbers fall off as the potential market becomes saturated. Some of those customers who have already been acquired will continue buying, but many will not. The number of newly acquired customers and the revenue associated with them will inevitably drop off as time goes on. This is true no matter what business you're analyzing, and it must be taken into account when looking at the future health and valuation of any company.

A 2017 research study by Wharton professor Marshall Fisher (with coauthors Vishal Gaur and Herb Kleinberger) analyzed 37 US retailers that had sold $1 billion or more but were past their growth phase (i.e., each had growth rates in the single digits). The study found that the less successful retailers among them were those that continued to chase growth at all costs, while the more successful retailers were those able to drastically change course by curtailing expansion and instead pour their efforts into driving additional sales and profit at existing stores. Here's how they described the larger corporate context in a *Harvard Business Review* article that distilled the trio's analysis:

> First, Wall Street and the capitalist culture celebrate—and demand—growth. Indeed, slow growth is regarded as something between a disease and a moral failing. When faced with declining growth, companies are urged to go back to the drawing board, rethink the business, and come up with a new strategy to pump up the top line. Second, leaders of many retail chains don't know when to make the transition. Consequently, they keep expanding until their chains begin to collapse under their own weight. And third, growth companies and mature businesses require very different operating strategies. Many companies that excel at growth lack the capabilities to make the switch.[92]

Retailers aren't the only ones who are guilty of acquisition addiction. Software as a service (SaaS) has recently been gaining popularity in the global marketplace, boasting a 20% growth rate in 2017 (bringing its current estimated worth as an industry up to $46 billion[93]). Given that this is a technology-based industry with easy access to lots of data about its customers, you'd think SaaS companies would know better than to be overly focused on acquisition. Think again.

Price Intelligently, a company dedicated to providing data-driven expertise and guidance to SaaS companies, conducted a survey of 1,218 SaaS CEOs in 2016. Each leader was asked how they would distribute 100 units of time across acquisition, monetization (developing existing customers to be worth more, which we discussed in chapter 3), and retention efforts within their company. Predictably, acquisition far eclipsed the other tactics, accounting for nearly 75% of the units, with a mere 20% allocated for retention and 5% tossed at monetization.[94]

Considering their marketplace is increasingly crowded with competitors that drive up acquisition costs, isn't it more logical for these companies to redirect their limited resources toward retaining their *existing* highest-value customers, and then maybe work harder to understand *which* of these existing customers potentially has additional value?

But let's bring this discussion full circle before we close. Recall the adage that we discussed before: It costs [X] times more to acquire a new customer than to retain an existing one, so you should focus on the ones you already have. The point we raised in the previous paragraph, in contrast to our discussion earlier in the book, seems to support such a viewpoint. Are we contradicting ourselves? No. The key words to solve this puzzle should be evident to astute (and customer-centric) readers: *highest-value customers*. The problem with that old adage is that too many companies follow it blindly without regard for the CLV of those customers that they are desperate to retain. But when a company is smart about acquisition (and CLV), it will have a better idea about the trade-offs between acquisition and retention (and development), and it will carefully align them with life-cycle dynamics and other market forces much more effectively than a company that views its customers largely as faceless, nameless, interchangeable entities.

The bottom line here is that investors should be doing the same thing. They should hold companies accountable in a similar manner and should reward those that can demonstrate genuine lasting value through the careful measurement of customer equity and the thoughtful deployment of customer-centric tactics.

Chapter Summary

- Traditional approaches to corporate valuation account for only the equity derived from financial and operational assets. They do not account for BE or CE. BE refers to the faith that customers have in a brand, and strong brand equity can boost a company in ways beyond simply products bought. CE is the sum of all present—and ideally, *future*—customer CLVs. Strong CE means better customers acquired more efficiently, longer customer relationships, and higher individual CLVs.

- Despite the difficulty in measuring BE, branding should be seen as the "lubrication of the customer centricity engine." The majority of BE can arise from and be measured through CLV, which means BE is, in essence, a component of CE. When customer acquisition becomes an unhealthy obsession as part of CBCV, it can lead to a company facing a horde of low-value customers who churn quickly—which tanks a company's value.

- As part of a customer-centric strategy, companies must align customer acquisition, retention, and development strategies with the company's maturity phase.

Chapter 6

Agile Change Management and Customer Centricity

We've now discussed the strategic and tactical frameworks and tools necessary for you to create and enact a customer-centric strategy. This chapter now shifts to the vital role that authoring a comprehensive strategic plan plays in successfully achieving customer centricity. We will touch on the scaffolding for this strategy that's provided by the organization itself—in particular, the alignment and maturity of an organization's mission, culture, leadership, structure, and processes.

Organizations that successfully adopt innovative approaches such as customer centricity are those that can navigate change with agility and minimal friction. It's easy to be myopic when we think about organizations that have achieved transformative change and to focus exclusively on the visionary leadership of the C-suite. Admittedly, most of our examples in this book are about such individuals, because leadership is so visible. But transformation never happens in a vacuum, and like EA's story demonstrates, it doesn't always begin at the top.

Here we'd like to recognize that *transformation* is just a sexier way of describing *change*. And to do change well, you need a plan, and a comprehensive one at that—a strategic plan. Executing such a plan following a best-practice framework is a common path for product-centric organizations, with numerous maturity and change management methodologies that are designed to maximize

product development, production, support, and sales. To name a few:

- manufacturing's Deming Cycle
- technology's Agile Methodology
- the Lean Startup Methodology
- ITIL's Continuous Service Improvement practice

All these approaches start by defining an action plan that delivers against a set of well-defined goals with incremental milestones. These goals must pass the SMART[95] test: They must be specific, measurable, achievable, relevant, and time-limited. Unsurprisingly, these iterative frameworks seem to have a lot of overlap with each other when viewed side by side, as shown in Figure 6.1.

Importantly, these frameworks are designed to be quick cycles (weeks in length, not months or years) where, in simplified terms, each cycle has a discovery and planning phase that defines a concise set of deliverables, which are then actioned and quality-checked. Finally, the team reflects on the cycle that just happened, usually with the project stakeholders, to help inform the direction of the next cycle.

An iterative approach is essential to change—and ultimately transformation—because it allows for minor course corrections to happen along the way, such as adjusting priorities, refining deliverables, and allowing breathing room in the plan to add new deliverables that weren't originally considered (which is inevitable).

Adapting the Agile Methodology for Customer Centricity

Although these methodologies were all developed in support of product-centric goals, we believe best practices like these can easily be adapted to support an organization moving to enact a customer-centric strategy. Being that Sarah's expertise is in Agile, we're going to take a deeper dive into adapting this particular methodology,

Figure 6.1. Comparison of Deming Cycle, Agile Methodology, Lean Startup Methodology, and ITIL's Continuous Service Improvement Practice

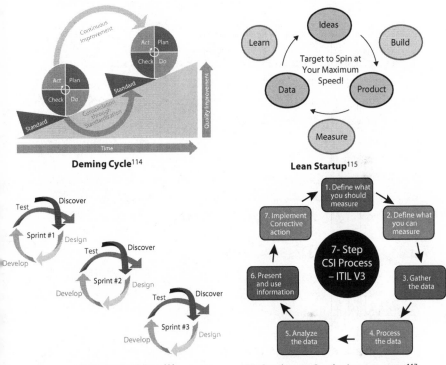

Sources: "Plan-Do-Check-Act (PDCA)," ConceptDraw, www.conceptdraw.com/solution-park/management-plan-do-check-act, accessed October 18, 2017; "Everything You Need to Know about the Lean Startup," AgileLeanLife, December 27, 2017, agileleanlife.com/the-lean-startup/; Michael Reich, "Agile v. Waterfall: How to Approach Your Web Development Project," Commonplaces Interactive (blog), www.commonplaces.com/blog/agile-v-waterfall-how-to-approach-your-web-development-project/, accessed October 18, 2017; Barcenas Cruz, "ITIL 101 for Dummies," LinkedIn, July 15, 2015, www.linkedin.com/pulse/itil-101-dummies-francisco-frank-barcenas-cruz.

but we urge you to look at the change and project management processes you're most comfortable with and undertake a similar process.

A Manifesto for Customer Centricity

Agile started in 2001 when several technologists became fed up with the convoluted, bloated processes used at the time for software development projects. These technologists decided to publish their revolutionary *Manifesto for Agile Software Development*[96]: a bold proclamation that launched radically new approaches to how software—and now technology and products in general—is developed and maintained. The manifesto sent a powerful message, shining a light on what *should* be the focus during a project rather than all the busywork that takes away from being able to be focused, to be lean, and to communicate effectively with project stakeholders. Today, if you're not lean and agile in the technology and product development fields, you're irrelevant.

This major shift in the collective mindset of an entire industry all started with this manifesto, which goes like this:

> We are uncovering better ways of developing software by doing it and helping others do it. Through this work we have come to value:
> **Individuals and Interactions** over processes and tools
> **Working Software** over comprehensive documentation
> **Customer Collaboration** over contract negotiation
> **Responding to Change** over following a plan
> That is, while there is value in the items on the right, we value the items on the left more.[97]

That got us thinking: What would a manifesto for customer centricity look like? So, we came up with our own (and if you'd like to add your name as a signatory, go to customercentricitymanifesto.org):

By wholly valuing, investing in, adopting, and endorsing items on the left we aim to develop and implement winning strategies that best leverage customer lifetime value:

Customer Heterogeneity over the Average Customer

Cross-Functional Uses of CLV over siloed applications

Metrics That Reflect Customer Equity over volume and cost obsession

Clear Communications with External Stakeholders over misalignment and misunderstanding

Customer Heterogeneity

Throughout this book—and extending back to the central discussion in Peter's first book and before—our mantra has been the importance of celebrating customer heterogeneity. This tenet of customer centricity is a realistic view of the world, and is one that seeks to capture, understand, and build action in tune with these naturally occurring variances.

Back in the late 1940s and 1950s when marketing (more or less as we think of it today) emerged as a way for product-centric firms to keep demand in line with supply, businesses started to notice that their customers were inherently different from one another. This discovery was a nuisance because it meant that one-size-fits-all approaches to marketing, while efficient on their face, are actually not as effective. Thankfully, there has been a 180 in thinking since those times, to the point where now we see strategies seizing on these differences to best leverage customer value—and to achieve sustainable growth that product-centric thinking may not be able to achieve.

A number of years ago, Peter worked with a small manufacturing company whose CEO truly believed in customer centricity. But the CEO grew frustrated by his staff who remained frozen in a product-centric mindset and habitually referred to "the" customer. So the CEO came up with a clever way to call attention to this bad habit. He placed a fishbowl at the front desk, and anytime someone in the company referred to "the" customer, they had to put a dollar in the bowl. It was a simple but very visible way to bring this important point across, day after day. Employees started listening carefully for the offending words, and there was always a lot of lighthearted buzz around the office whenever anyone would catch someone saying them. Then, at the end of the year, the CEO used those funds (with some more of his own) for a "Celebration of Customer Heterogeneity" party. What a great way to move the conversation forward around this important concept!

Cross-Functional Uses of CLV

An effective and accessible way to move the needle in your organization is to not only use the right words about customer centricity but turn them into broad actions. Specifically, a truly customer-centric firm will seek to establish a variety of use cases across the organization that demonstrate the strategic advantages that a focus on CLV (and related predictive analytics) can provide. This is one of the reasons EA has found such success in recent years—it actively looks for new and different ways to create mission-critical applications of CLV. Not only does this help the company maintain a forward-looking perspective on its business, but it also creates common ground to evaluate those initiatives across seemingly unrelated functional areas within the organization.

According to Peter, this was one of his greatest joys in running Zodiac: Besides the standard acquisition/retention/development use cases (e.g., determining which email to send to which customer at which time), many clients would dream up new use cases that Peter and colleagues hadn't thought of themselves. Examples include salesforce compensation/incentives, new product evaluation (based on the CLV of customers who try it), promotional campaign evaluation, and providing guidance to research and development teams to help them dream up products that will best appeal to high-value customers. And of course there's the idea of customer-based corporate valuation to win over the finance and accounting staff.

In general, it is essential to get cross-functional buy-in for customer centricity (or any strategy) to succeed, and there is no better way to do so than to make its incentive compatible for as many employees as possible to embrace CLV and begin to work with each other to best leverage it.

Metrics That Reflect Customer Equity

The leading customer metric used by businesses today is Net Promoter Score (NPS). Although many academics dislike its simplicity (compared with much more elaborate measures that countless professors have conjured up over the years), we really like the fact that by taking the difference between the fraction of "promoters" and "detractors," NPS celebrates heterogeneity. As we have said countless times in these pages, the spread across customers is at least as interesting and important as the average.

So, in this sense, NPS is a natural starting point to get senior executives to understand and appreciate customer centricity, but it might not be the "ultimate" metric, as Fred Reichheld suggested when he wrote his hugely popular book and other publications on the topic.[98]

Nevertheless, tapping into the spirit of NPS, we want to see firms adopt a broader set of metrics that directly or indirectly reflect customers' propensities to be acquired, buy repeatedly, maintain the relationship, refer others, respond to the right messages, and so on. We know these propensities are latent and deeply intertwined, making efforts to study them more complex and error prone. We believe that by starting with the true ultimate metric—corporate valuation— then working backward to CLV and its underlying components, more clarity can be brought to the important decision of which metrics to rely on to evaluate and communicate the effectiveness of a customer-centric strategy.

Most firms are in the very early stages of using these metrics internally (we'll get to external uses in a moment), so it's important to take these first steps in a careful manner. In some of his aforementioned work with Dan McCarthy on customer-based corporate valuation, Peter has looked at various metrics that firms occasionally report (sometimes informally, other times in more formal financial statements). These include some fairly self-explanatory metrics such as *quarterly total orders* and *quarterly active users*, as well as some more complex ones, for example, *percentage of current orders arising from repeat-buying customers*. It is very important for firms to understand how these and other emerging metrics relate to CLV (and, through customer equity, to corporate valuation). First and foremost, this exercise should be done for internal purposes: Going back to the cross-functional use cases just discussed, which aggregate metrics to best reflect the effectiveness of each of these activities? Obviously a firm doesn't want to overcomplicate its performance scorecard, but executives will surely need an array of customer metrics to reflect the different ways that CLV (and customer centricity in general) is creating value across the organization.

And once these metrics are established for internal usage, it's then time to win over the external stakeholders, which is our final point in the manifesto.

Clear Communication with External Partners

Most companies have a major disconnect between the way they strive for long-run growth and the manner in which they are held accountable by short-term financial metrics. This is one of the biggest limiting factors of product-centric thinking, which often puts volume maximization and cost minimization ahead of other activities (and metrics) that may be more closely associated with long-term value creation for high-value customers. A perfect example of this disconnect was covered in the discussion about "acquisition addiction" in chapter 5: Is a given company growing via healthy, sustained means where customers are staying and buying repeatedly, or is the company growing only through newly acquired customers, who then leave quickly? It's obvious that a company would want to use the right internal metrics to diagnose such an issue and take action on it as quickly as possible. But shouldn't external stakeholders want to do the same?

We believe that customer centricity can create this kind of natural alignment to get internal and external stakeholders to agree on metrics that are helpful for day-to-day operational purposes as well as the evaluation of a firm's long-run health. That's the beauty of focusing on a forward-looking metric like CLV—it is the right ingredient to achieve both goals. We're already seeing a number of venture capital firms and even some private equity shops that use a CLV metric to help in their diligence process for prospective investments and also to compare the ongoing performance of their existing portfolio companies. This is a very promising sign and, as noted earlier, is the main focus of Peter's new firm (Theta Equity Partners).

Of course, it is very early days for external stakeholders to rely on customer metrics to do their jobs, but times are changing in this regard, and we believe that a day will come when external people and firms not only begin to deeply understand such metrics but also start to demand them. Who knows, maybe one day the accounting standards agencies in the United States and other countries will regulate the definition and use of them. OK, we admit that such a step would be a generation away, at best, but that shouldn't stop firms from trying to educate their external stakeholders about customer-centric metrics and practices now.

In a similar way, Agile took decades to take root and gain widespread adoption. Even before the 2001 Agile Manifesto was published, there was a groundswell of activity in the software field that attempted to make existing practices less burdensome. For example, Scrum's iterative process was launched in the 1990s and is now the gold standard for how to enact the points laid out in the manifesto.[99]

Agility Leads to Successful Transformation

We're not going to get into granular detail here about Agile, but it is worthwhile to take a brief look at how Agile can be adapted to support developing and implementing a customer-centric strategy. Sprints are a central mechanism of Scrum, a form of Agile we mentioned briefly above. In reviewing this methodology, as illustrated in Figure 6.1, sprints look a lot like gears and cogs, which in practice is how they should work too. At a high level, sprints

- are short, iterative cycles, where each sprint is composed of a set of related work tasks that, when complete, will achieve a succinct goal;
- happen sequentially; and
- drive the momentum of future sprints.[100]

Directly before a sprint begins, the team comes together with stakeholders to do sprint planning during the discovery phase. Here the delivery team defines the tasks of the sprint together, with the goal of making sure that the work that is delivered can stand on its own by the end of the sprint and be evaluated and tested at the component level.

The sprint then moves into the design phase, followed by the develop phase (essentially, the *doing the work* phases). During this active time, the team meets daily for a short stand-up, flagging issues for project managers whose job it is to clear barriers and ensure that the sprint is completed on time.

Last but not least, the review phase is where the sprint deliverables are assessed for completeness and quality, usually with stakeholders. Moving into the next sprint is where the magic of this process happens, because future discovery phases are informed by those sprints that happened before, allowing stakeholders to continually check the thoroughness and priorities of their own requirements against what is coming to life in the delivery.

Adapting this process to develop a customer-centric plan means that goals of the delivery must shift from the *product* to the *customer* in all the ways we have described in this book so far. Using the Manifesto for Customer Centricity as a guidepost, and underpinned by an iterative process like Agile, the plan should

- develop and validate CLV models;
- use profiling based on CLV to improve precision;
- run CLV-based experiments for acquisition, retention, and development tactics (recall the 2×2 frameworks we discussed in chapters 2 and 3);
- align organizational priorities to maximize value; and
- develop metrics to best capture, measure, and convey the effectiveness of the program.

To see this approach in action, let's take a look at the Los Angeles Dodgers, which followed a similar plan to the one outlined here, and is another customer centricity success story.

The Los Angeles Dodgers Case: A Home Run for Customer Centricity

In 2012, when Guggenheim Baseball Management arrived as the new ownership group for the Dodgers, things were far from perfect. Even though the Dodgers are fortunate to have a devoted fan base and the second largest market in the sport, Forbes had listed their revenues back then as tied for sixth in Major League Baseball.[101] The new ownership group got to work right away on transforming the team and the business, pulling off blockbuster player trades and investing heavily into the fan experience at Dodger Stadium. With an eye toward building for the future, they have also been among the most aggressive sports franchises to develop analytics functions on and off the field.

Royce Cohen, now vice president of business development and analytics for the Dodgers, is fanatical about two things: baseball and data.[102] If there were a sequel to *Moneyball*—but this time centered around customer stats rather than player stats—there's no doubt Cohen's story could easily be the main theme. These joint passions led him to intern twice for the San Francisco Giants during college, and then after graduation to take a position with Major League Baseball in analytics. A few short years later, he landed his dream position with the Los Angeles Dodgers, where he has risen quickly through the ranks.

When Cohen joined the team in 2014 and looked around for opportunities to improve the business, he was struck by the absence of an enterprise CRM, and that ticket sales were mostly managed using Excel.

On the bright side, the lack of sophisticated business intelligence systems presented opportunities for the Dodgers to build an analytics stack from scratch in a way that was system agnostic. Cohen shared in a recent conversation that "this forced us to think about the problems we want to solve with data in a way that isn't dictated by the system we want to work in."

One of the earliest projects for the business analytics team was an ambitious CLV segmentation study. While the data teams at most baseball organizations were leaning on the observable characteristics of their customers, like personas and demographics that we warned against in chapter 2, Cohen believed strongly in the approaches Peter was proving out in study after study about CLV. Unfortunately, this first attempt wasn't the smashing success Cohen had hoped it would be because he and the team faced a myriad of challenges relating to limited historical data about customers. But they persisted in this vein, building out the data warehouses, analytics, and other business intelligence infrastructure that were required to model CLV effectively, and now with five extra years of rich customer data, they have been able to realize their original vision.

As Cohen explains, the business of ticketing is commonly summed up by three questions: "How many tickets will sell? At what price? And in response to which promotions?" He has been on a mission to add a fourth question: "To which customers?"

Once you have reliable models that accurately reflect the heterogeneous makeup of your customers—which the Dodgers now have and rely on—it's easier to analyze these tightly linked questions in integrated ways, and thus better understand the varying propensities of your customers with respect to buying and price points.

In practice, confidence in these models has translated into numerous innovations for the Dodgers' various acquisition, retention, and development tactics. For instance, this year they launched a new two-tiered early season ticket renewal offering. The first tier is aimed to further develop the value of their longest-standing, highest-paying customers who are proven to be loyal, less price sensitive, and thus happy to pay extra for their season tickets in exchange for a number of desirable benefits (like batting practice on the field and deals at the concession stand). On the other hand, the second tier skews more heavily to season ticket holders who have had seats for less than 10 years and may be paying a lower-average price per seat. For this tier, the main additional perk is offering the same price for the following year, making this more of a retention play.

The results of the Dodgers' improved business strategies are best reflected in the numbers. In the past five years, the team has doubled revenues, moving up to second place in the earnings leaderboard for the league, as illustrated in Figure 6.2.[103]

Figure 6.2. Revenue of the Los Angeles Dodgers, 2001–2017 (millions of US dollars)

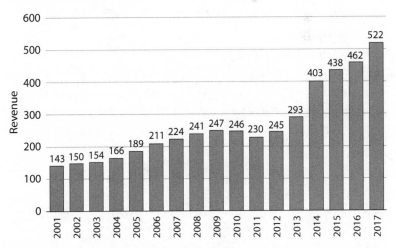

Source: "Revenue of the Los Angeles Dodgers (MLB) from 2001 to 2017 (in million U.S. dollars)," Statista, www.statista.com/statistics/196665/revenue-of-the-los-angeles-dodgers/, accessed August 10, 2018.

Even more remarkable, as the Dodgers improved the scalability and robustness of their CLV models, and saw the impressive rise in revenue as a result, they realized that they had developed a winning approach that can be transferred to any business. This realization led them to launch the Global Sports Venture Studio, a platform that aims to "help partners tap into innovation by understanding relevant technologies, business models, and consumer behaviors—and the ways in which they overlap."[104] With more than 30 portfolio and partner companies to date, this new venture will very likely prove to be a viable business model for many years to come.

Chapter Summary

- You can leverage an iterative, best-practice framework to help you create a transformative plan for a customer-centric strategy. The Agile methodology is especially apt for this process.
- The Manifesto for Customer Centricity—based on the Manifesto for Agile Software Development—celebrates customer heterogeneity, cross-functional uses of CLV, metrics that reflect customer equity, and clear communication with external stakeholders.
- Drawing on Agile or another iterative, best-practice framework will help leaders regularly collect and analyze performance data during a customer-centric transformation, provide opportunities for consistent and transparent communication, and gain buy-in across the organization.

Conclusion
Customer Centricity from Concept to Playbook to Action

Although Peter's first book was titled *Customer Centricity: Focus on the Right Customers for Strategic Advantage*, his working title while writing the book was "Customer Centricity: What It Is, What It Isn't, and Why It Matters." That language reflected the fact that it was written during the early days of customer-centric thinking; the key objective at the time was simply to get managers to understand what those words mean and how they differ from product centricity. We've had to repeat some of those initial lessons here, naturally, but for the most part we've assumed that you now understand and appreciate what customer centricity is (and isn't), and instead are much more interested in getting such a strategy off the ground. That's why we chose to call this book a "playbook": You need to get moving with specific tactics instead of waiting on the sidelines and contemplating when (or even whether) to get in the game.

We're pleased to see that the business world has learned a lot in the years since Peter's first book came out. It's much easier to find successful case studies of customer-centric companies, or at least serious efforts toward customer-centric transformation that are now under way. Countless companies are in the early stages as they set up the right data infrastructure and organizational components and embark on the specific marketing and operational tactics that we have outlined here. A quick reread of that earlier book makes this contrast clear: Peter highlighted five companies (Nordstrom, Apple, Starbucks, Costco, and Walmart) that were often regarded as customer centric, but he pointed out why they failed to meet the specific definition that he proposed, which we have shared in chapter 1. Peter is now the first to admit that all five of them have made some excellent strides in this direction over the years since he laid out his initial doubts about their true commitment to customer centricity.

But there are no guarantees here. Simply following a playbook doesn't ensure long-term success. Of course we want to end our book on a constructive, positive note, but before we do, it is useful to review the stories of customer-centric "heroes" that encountered some bumps in the road.

Two Cautionary Tales

Two of the most highlighted companies in Peter's first book were Harrah's (the casino chain that, through its customer-centric success, merged with and took the name of Caesar's Entertainment) and Tesco (the UK-based grocery chain). We won't repeat the original stories here, but both rose through the ranks of their respective industries by embracing customer-level data, celebrating heterogeneity, and aligning many of their activities around the creation of value for their most valuable customers. They became the envy of all firms in both sectors and the subjects of many business school case study discussions.

However, in the years since they found world-class success by epitomizing customer-centric brilliance, both have stumbled for a variety of reasons. One reason in both cases is that the competition didn't simply sit by and allow Caesar's and Tesco to run away with their markets. Instead, competitors started to emulate some of the successful strategies and tactics that they had been observing and used their deeper pockets (which originally drove Caesar's and Tesco to differentiate themselves by moving in the customer-centric direction in the first place) to beat out focal firms at their own game. Additionally, both "doubled down" on their success with ambitious expansion plans that led to some financial distress.

But these are merely cautionary tales, not failure stories. Both firms are doing reasonably well today, even though they are no longer achieving the meteoric success (or receiving the endless respect from customers, investors, and competitors) that characterized them around 2011. Times change, and strategies and tactics must change along with them.

This is where the "playbook" idea comes in: In any sporting event, it is not enough to run a successful series of plays and then to declare victory. Competitors adjust, game conditions change, and the apparent "magic" that accompanied the good run seems to evaporate. That's why it's essential to think several plays ahead, to anticipate that tactics will have to shift as part of a forward-looking strategy. Tomorrow's focal customers might be a different group from today's, or the effectiveness of certain acquisition channels might change because of oversaturation or changes in costs (owing, perhaps, to your own past successes in those channels). Even the companies that we praised at the outset of this book (EA and Best Buy) will eventually stumble, but we hope that they will have thought enough about these inevitable dynamics that they will be prepared to adjust as needed.

From Playbook to Action

Even though a playbook is more action-oriented than a strictly conceptual overview, it is still just a series of plans. Yes, it's more concrete and tactical, and (as just mentioned) it should prepare you for some unexpected changes in the marketplace. But at some point, it's time to stop planning and to start doing. There is no better way to learn about the best future plans than to see what actually works and what doesn't.

Obviously, this applies to customer centricity as much as any other endeavor in life—maybe even more so, because it is such an unfamiliar way of doing business for so many firms. This is where a good simulation comes in. We are both strong advocates for using a well-designed simulation for learning purposes: Peter frequently uses business simulations as a compelling experiential teaching device in his classes, and Sarah's main role at Wharton is to develop them and help faculty be as effective as possible by using them.

As we noted earlier in the book, we collaborated to develop a new simulation for one of Peter's courses. In many ways, that experience catalyzed the thought process for this book, but it's also interesting to understand how the pedagogical role of the simulation itself has also changed over the years of its development. As noted earlier, the sim used to be a "capstone" exercise, coming at the end of Peter's course, intended to tie together all the concepts and lessons that he had covered over the semester. But, more recently, we have found even greater success by leading with the sim instead of using it as a wrap-up exercise. Let's throw participants right into the water and teach them to swim in real time—albeit in a simulated environment where no one can actually drown. There is a lot to be said for letting experience drive the creation of future plans. At the end of the game, participants are eager to learn, and they have a much greater contextual appreciation for the kinds of details that we have laid out in the pages of this book. There really is a lot to be said for getting to action very quickly, and letting actual (or simulated) experience drive the creation of future plans.

We don't want to suggest that this book is the final word on this topic—quite to the contrary, there is *much* more to be learned and shared about the right ways to approach customer centricity. The strategy has to be a living process, one that is continually tested, verified, and improved. At the same time, we believe the world has reached an important step in this evolving process. Early success stories have matured, new ones are just coming into view, and the best are likely yet to come. One day, customer-centric strategies will be seen as standard options in the business world, not as radical departures from today's omnipresent product-centric thinking.

In the preface to this book, we used the metaphor of Michael Phelps to convey the idea that good customers are basically born good. However, we can describe a specimen such as Phelps all day long, and some readers will still be (rightfully) skeptical about whether those physical attributes alone will translate into world-class speed in the pool—or, in the case of customers, a high CLV. The bottom line is this: You just have to find and watch your customers in the water to find out. We can motivate you, help you plan, lay out contingencies, and so on, but at some point, you have to just start the work. For customer centricity, that time is now.

Notes

1   "Electronic Arts on the Forbes Global 2000 List," *Forbes*, June 2018, www.forbes
    .com/companies/electronic·arts/.

2   Paul Tassi, "EA Voted Worst Company in America, Again," *Forbes*, April 19,
    2013, www.forbes.com/sites/insertcoin/2013/04/09/ea-voted-worst-company-in
    -america-again/.

3   "Electronic Arts Inc. (EA) Interactive Chart," Nasdaq, July 16, 2018, www
    .nasdaq.com/symbol/ea/interactive-chart. From mid-2012 to mid-2018, stock
    values have jumped from about $12/share to about $140/share.

4   Peter Wells, "EA Jumps on Strong Revenue Growth in 2017," *Financial Times*,
    January 30, 2018, www.ft.com/content/caeafb9a-0605-11e8-9650-9c0ad2d7c5b5.

5   Benjamin Tisdale, senior director of business analytics at EA, interview by the
    author, July 13, 2018.

6   Tisdale, interview.

7   "Electronic Arts Reports Q4 FY17 and Full Year FY17 Financial Results,"
    Electronic Arts, May 9, 2017, investor.ea.com/releasedetail.cfm?ReleaseID
    =1025604.

8   Peter Fader, *Customer Centricity: Focus on the Right Customers for Strategic
    Advantage* (Philadelphia: Wharton Digital Press, 2012), p. 39.

9   *Products* throughout this book refers to products or services.

10 Charisse Jones and Chris Woodyard, "Which Stores Is Rue21 Closing? Here's a
    List," *USA Today*, April 19, 2017, www.usatoday.com/story/money/business/2017
    /04/19/which-stores-rue21-closing-heres-many-them/100616484/.

11 Barbara Farfan, "Here Is a List of the Macy's Stores Going out of Business in
    2017," The Balance, October 9, 2017, www.thebalance.com/macys-store-closings
    -2892434.

12 Josh Sanburn, "Why the Death of Malls Is More than Shopping," *Time*, July 20,
    2017, time.com/4865957/death-and-life-shopping-mall/.

13 "Get Bespoke's Most Actionable Ideas," Bespoke Investment Group, April 13,
    2017, www.bespokepremium.com/?s=Death%2Bby%2Bamazon.

14 Fred Imbert, "New ProShares ETF Makes Money When Retail Stocks Get Hit,"
    CNBC, November 24, 2017, www.cnbc.com/2017/11/24/decline-of-the-retail
    -store-etf-tries-to-make-money-off-retails-misery.html.

15 "Best Buy (BBY): 33 Year Stock Price History," MacroTrends, March 9, 2018, www.macrotrends.net/stocks/charts/BBY/prices/best-buy-stock-price-history.

16 Jen Wieczner, "Meet the Women Who Saved Best Buy: The Exclusive Story," *Fortune*, October 25, 2015, fortune.com/2015/10/25/best-buy-turnaround/.

17 Kevin Roose, "Best Buy's Secrets for Thriving in the Amazon Age," *New York Times*, September 18, 2017, www.nytimes.com/2017/09/18/business/best-buy -amazon.html.

18 Ranjay Gulati, "Inside Best Buy's Customer-Centric Strategy," *Harvard Business Review*, July 23, 2014, hbr.org/2010/04/inside-best-buys-customer-cent.

19 For a primer on the IoT, see Jacob Morgan's "A Simple Explanation of 'The Internet of Things,'" *Forbes*, May 13, 2014, https://www.forbes.com/sites /jacobmorgan/2014/05/13/simple-explanation-internet-things-that-anyone-can -understand/#725a2f151d09.

20 Michael Shirer, "New IDC Smart Home Device Tracker Forecasts Solid Growth for Connected Devices in Key Smart Home Categories," *IDC: The Premier Global Market Intelligence Company*, March 29, 2018, www.idc.com/getdoc.jsp ?containerId=prUS43701518.

21 Casey Coombs, "Amazon Takes Aim at Best Buy with Technology House Calls," *Puget Sound Business Journal*, July 10, 2017, www.bizjournals.com /seattle/news/2017/07/10/amazon-smart-home-technology-house-calls-best -buy.html.

22 Larry Dignan, "Nike's Purchase of Analytics Firm Zodiac Highlights Focus on Customer Lifetime Value," ZDNet, March 23, 2018, http://zd.net/2pBuUlO.

23 Peter Fader and Bruce Hardie, "Reconciling and Clarifying CLV Formulas," Faculty Website: Bruce Hardie, March 2012, brucehardie.com/notes/024 /reconciling_clv_formulas.pdf; Peter Fader and Bruce Hardie, "What's Wrong with This CLV Formula?," Faculty Website: Bruce Hardie, December 2014, brucehardie.com/notes/033/what_is_wrong_with_this_CLV_formula.pdf.

24 P. E. Pfeifer, M. E. Haskins, and R. M. Conroy, "Customer Lifetime Value, Customer Profitability, and the Treatment of Acquisition Spending," *Journal of Managerial Issues* 17, no. 1 (2005): 17.

25 Fader and Hardie, "Reconciling and Clarifying CLV Formulas"; Fader and Hardie, "What's Wrong with This CLV Formula?"

26 Peter S. Fader and Bruce G. S. Hardie, "Customer-Base Valuation in a Contractual Setting: The Perils of Ignoring Heterogeneity," *Marketing Science* 29 (January–February 2010): 91.

27 Fader and Hardie, "What's Wrong with This CLV Formula?," p. 4.

28 Byron Sharp and Charles Graham, "The Value of Pareto's Bottom 80%," Ehrenberg-Bass Institute for Marketing Science, January 26, 2018, www .marketingscience.info/value-paretos-bottom-80/; Byron Sharp, *How Brands Grow: What Marketers Don't Know* (Oxford: Oxford University Press, 2016).

29 Dwight McNeill, *A Framework for Applying Analytics in Healthcare: What Can Be Learned from the Best Practices in Retail, Banking, Politics, and Sports* (Upper Saddle River, NJ: FT Press, 2013), p. 76.

30 Wikipedia, s.v. "Jeff Bezos," last modified August 14, 2018, en.wikipedia.org /wiki/Jeff_Bezos#Amazon.com.

31 Lauren Thomas, "Amazon's Market Cap Is Now Worth Almost Twice That of Wal-Mart," CNBC, April 5, 2017, www.cnbc.com/2017/04/05/amazon-worth -twice-wal-mart.html.

32 George Packer, "Cheap Words: Amazon Is Good for Customers but Is It Good for Books?," *New Yorker*, February 17, 2014, www.newyorker.com/magazine /2014/02/17/cheap-words.

33 Matthew Yglesias, "The Prophet of No Profit," Slate, January 31, 2014, www.slate .com/articles/business/moneybox/2014/01/amazon_earnings_how_jeff_bezos _gets_investors_to_believe_in_him.html.

34 Frederick F. Reichheld and Thomas Teal, *The Loyalty Effect: The Hidden Force behind Growth, Profits, and Lasting Value* (Boston: Harvard Business School Press, 2008). Reichheld, a senior consultant at Bain, gained even more fame a few years later when he introduced Net Promoter Score to the business world.

35 Fader, *Customer Centricity*, p. 50.

36 The authors thank Professor Renana Peres of the Hebrew University of Jerusalem for codeveloping a version of this grid with Peter as part of a course that they co-taught at Wharton.

37 As a result of the demand for large databases of leads, the list-broker business has become a giant, multibillion-dollar industry where brokers work as the middle person between companies that are seeking specific sets of leads and list sellers who hold vast quantities of individual prospects. See Craig Simpson, "How to Work with a Mailing List Broker," *Entrepreneur*, March 9, 2017, www .entrepreneur.com/article/287359.

38 "Lookalike Audiences," Facebook, www.facebook.com/business/a/lookalike -audiences, accessed July 17, 2018.

39 Shawndra Hill, Foster Provost, and Chris Volinsky, "Network-Based Marketing: Identifying Likely Adopters via Consumer Networks," *Statistical Science* 21, no. 2 (2006): 256, doi:10.1214/088342306000000222.

40 Philipp Schmitt, Bernd Skiera, and Christophe Van Den Bulte, "Why Customer Referrals Can Drive Stunning Profits," *Harvard Business Review*, June 1, 2011, hbr .org/2011/06/why-customer-referrals-can-drive-stunning-profits; Christophe Van Den Bulte, Emanuel Bayer, Bernd Skiera, and Phillipp Schmitt, "How Customer Referral Programs Turn Social Capital into Economic Capital," *Journal of Marketing Research* 55, no. 1 (February 2018): 132–146, doi:10.1509/jmr.14.0653.

41 Glenn Lawyer, "Understanding the Influence of All Nodes in a Network," *Nature News*, March 2, 2015, www.nature.com/articles/srep08665.

42 Barak Libai, Eitan Muller, and Renana Peres, "The Role of Seeding in Multi-market Entry," *International Journal in Research Marketing* 22 (2005): 375, doi:10.18411/d-2016-154.

43 Nagesh Belludi, "The Drunkard's Search or the Streetlight Effect [Cognitive Bias]," Right Attitudes, February 26, 2016, www.rightattitudes.com/2016/02/26/drunkard-search-streetlight-effect/.

44 Mark Walston, "A Brief History of Chevrolet Advertising," Mark Walston, October 21, 2015, markwalston.com/2015/09/06/a-brief-history-of-chevrolet-advertising/.

45 Jack Doyle, "Dinah Shore & Chevrolet, 1951–1963," The Pop History Dig, March 22, 2009, www.pophistorydig.com/topics/dinah-shore-chevrolet-1950s-1960s/.

46 Doyle, "Dinah Shore & Chevrolet."

47 Denish Shah, V. Kumar, Yingge Qu, and Sylia Chen, "Unprofitable Cross-Buying: Evidence from Consumer and Business Markets," *Journal of Marketing* 76, no. 3 (May 2012): 78–95, doi:10.1509/jm.10.0445.

48 Denish Shah and V. Kumar, "The Dark Side of Cross-Selling," *Harvard Business Review*, December 2012, hbr.org/2012/12/the-dark-side-of-cross-selling.

49 Steven M. Shugan, "Brand Loyalty Programs: Are They Shams?," *Marketing Science* 24, no. 2 (2005): 185–193, doi:10.1287/mksc.1050.0124; Grahame Dowling and Mark Uncles, "Do Customer Loyalty Programs Really Work?," *Sloan Management Review*, 1997, pp. 71–82.

50 Matthew Dollinger, "Starbucks, 'The Third Place,' and Creating the Ultimate Customer Experience," Fast Company, July 30, 2012, www.fastcompany.com/887990/starbucks-third-place-and-creating-ultimate-customer-experience, http://adage.com/article/guest-columnists/practices-a-customer-centric-company/301127/.

51 "Starbucks Mobile Order & Pay Now Available to Customers Nationwide," Starbucks Newsroom, press release, September 22, 2015, news.starbucks.com/news/starbucks-mobile-order-pay-now-available-to-customers-nationwide.

52 Trefis Team, "Starbucks' Success with Mobile Order and Pay Is Too Much of a Good Thing," *Forbes*, February 2, 2017, www.forbes.com/sites/greatspeculations/2017/02/02/starbucks-success-with-mobile-order-and-pay-is-too-much-of-a-good-thing/#380a8a7343da.

53 Hadley Malcolm, "Starbucks Loyalty Program Will Now Be Based on Dollars Spent," *USA Today*, February 22, 2016, www.usatoday.com/story/money/2016/02/22/starbucks-loyalty-program-changing-to-be-based-on-dollars-spent/80725784/.

54 Sharon Florentine and Matt Kapko, "Why LinkedIn Premium Is Worth the Money," CIO, July 27, 2017, www.cio.com/article/2877153/social-networking/why-linkedin-premium-is-worth-the-money.html.

55 LinkedIn Corporate Communications Team, "LinkedIn Announces Third
    Quarter 2016 Results," LinkedIn Newsroom, October 27, 2016, news.linkedin
    .com/2016/linkedin-announces-third-quarter-2016-results.

56 Kaya Yurieff, "LinkedIn Brings in Nearly $1 Billion in Revenue for Microsoft,"
    CNNMoney, April 27, 2017, money.cnn.com/2017/04/27/technology/microsoft
    -earnings/index.html.

57 "How Does LinkedIn (LNKD) Make Money?," Investopedia, December 2, 2014,
    www.investopedia.com/ask/answers/120214/how-does-linkedin-lnkd-make
    -money.asp.

58 Alexei Oreskovic, "Mark Zuckerberg Just Hinted That Facebook Could Offer a
    Paid Version One Day," Business Insider, April 10, 2018, www.businessinsider
    .com/mark-zuckerberg-always-a-version-of-facebook-free-2018-4.

59 Monster.com, https://www.monster.com/jobs/search/?q=strategic-account
    -manager; Indeed.com, https://www.indeed.com/jobs?q=strategic+account
    +manager&l=.

60 Mike Schultz, "6 Strategic Account Management Roles Every Company Needs to
    Know About," Sales Performance Improvement (blog), January 18, 2017, www
    .rainsalestraining.com/blog/6-account-management-roles.

61 "Autodesk, Inc. (ADSK) Interactive Chart," Nasdaq, www.nasdaq.com/symbol
    /adsk/interactive-chart, accessed July 17, 2018.

62 "Autodesk, Inc."

63 John P. Kelly, Jeff Kaplan, and Christine M. Larson., "How the Best Get Better:
    Seven Transformative Questions for Strategic Account Management," J Alan
    Group LLC, 2012, jalanconsulting.com/wp-content/uploads/2015/01/SAMA
    _Velocity_How-the-Best-Get-Better_Part-1.pdf. The authors are managing
    partners at Ferrazzi Greenlight, Inc.

64 Rob Markey and Fred Reichheld, "Introducing the Net Promoter System," Bain
    & Company, December 8, 2011, www.bain.com/publications/articles
    /introducing-the-net-promoter-system-loyalty-insights.aspx.

65 Joachim Buschken, Higher Profits through Customer Lock-in: A Roadmap (Mason,
    OH: Thomson, 2004); Thomas Burnham, Judy K. Frels, and Vijay Mahajan,
    "Customer Switching Costs: A Typology, Antecedents, and Consequences," Journal
    of the Academy of Marketing Sciences 31, no. 2 (2003): 109–126.

66 "What Is CRM?," Salesforce (blog), August 16, 2016, www.salesforce.com/blog
    /2013/01/what-is-crm-your-business-nerve-center.html.

67 "Interview with CRM Thought Leader Paul Greenberg," YouTube, July 6, 2016,
    www.youtube.com/watch?v=aUeSextjPr4.

68 EPN, "Evolution Web 1.0, Web 2.0 to Web 3.0," YouTube, September 28, 2008,
    www.youtube.com/watch?v=bsNcjya56v8#action=share.

69   Tamara Dull, "Data Lake vs. Data Warehouse: Key Differences," Kdnuggets, September 2015, www.kdnuggets.com/2015/09/data-lake-vs-data-warehouse-key -differences.html.

70   Arthur M. Hughes's book *Strategic Database Marketing: The Masterplan for Starting and Managing a Profitable, Customer-Based Marketing Program* covers nearly all, if not all, the major metrics and supporting calculations that professionals who interface with customer data should feel comfortable working with. Master the basic concepts covered by Hughes, along with the concepts in *this* book, and you'll be on your way to taking a wide variety of customer insights to the next level by using modern data analytics, visualization, and machine-learning techniques.

71   Tisdale, interview.

72   EA uses lifetime value (LTV), but the implementation details are identical to CLV, regardless of the label.

73   Elizabeth Gurdus, "Gap CEO Art Peck: Big Data Gives Us Major Advantages over Competitors," CNBC, April 11, 2018, www.cnbc.com/2018/04/11/gap-ceo -art-peck-big-data-gives-us-major-advantages-over-competitors.html.

74   "Cox Enterprises on the Forbes Best Employers for Diversity List," *Forbes*, December 31, 2016, www.forbes.com/companies/cox-enterprises/.

75   Gene Marks, "11 Terrible CRM Systems for Your Company," *Forbes*, July 1, 2013, www.forbes.com/sites/quickerbettertech/2013/07/01/11-terrible-crm-systems-for -your-company/.

76   David Reibstein, "House of Brands vs. Branded House," *Economist*, Global Agenda 3, 2005, pp. 175–177, https://www.researchgate.net/publication /262450255_House_of_Brands_vs_Branded_House.

77   Tim Koler, Mark Goedhardt, and David Wessels, *Valuation: University Edition*, 5th ed. (Hoboken, NJ: John Wiley & Sons, 2010). On page 821 of the index, under "C," there is a single reference to "customer lock-in," which refers to switching costs.

78   Aswath Damodaran, *The Little Book of Valuation: How to Value a Company, Pick a Stock, and Profit* (Hoboken, NJ: John Wiley & Sons, 2011). To Damodaran's credit, he has recently begun to embrace some of the elements of customer-based corporate valuation that we espouse here. See, e.g., Aswath Damodaran, *Going to Pieces: Valuing Users, Subscribers and Customers*, May 23, 2018, available at SSRN: https://ssrn.com/abstract=3175652.

79   C. Arkolakis, "Market Penetration Costs and the New Customers Margin in International Trade," *Journal of Political Economy* 118 (2010): 1151–1199.

80   Kurt Badenhausen, "Apple, Google Top the World's Most Valuable Brands of 2016," *Forbes*, May 11, 2016, www.forbes.com/sites/kurtbadenhausen/2016/05/11 /the-worlds-most-valuable-brands/#542f9a0a36ec.

81   Hal Conick, "Viral Video Tanks United Airlines Brand by Nearly $800 Million," American Marketing Association, April 11, 2017, www.ama.org/publications

/eNewsletters/Marketing-News-Weekly/Pages/viral-video-tanks-united-airlines
-brand-nearly-800-million.aspx.

82 Wikipedia, s.v. "Brand Equity," accessed April 24, 2018. en.wikipedia.org/wiki
/Brand_equity.

83 "Best Brands," Interbrand, December 2017, interbrand.com/best-brands/best
-global-brands/2017/ranking/.

84 Leena Rudanko, "The Value of Loyal Customers," *Federal Reserve Bank of
Philadelphia*, Q2 2017, www.philadelphiafed.org/-/media/research-and-data
/publications/economic-insights/2017/q2/eiq22017_loyalcustomers.pdf?la=en;
François Gourio and Leena Rudanko, "Customer Capital," *Review of Economic
Studies* 81 (2014): 1102–36; Thorsten Wiesel, Bernd Skiera, and Julian Villaneuva,
"Customer Equity: An Integral Part of Financial Reporting," *Journal of Marketing*
72, no. 2 (2008): 1–14, doi:10.1509/jmkg.72.2.1.

85 "What's the Difference between Bottom-Line and Top-Line Growth?,"
Investopedia, May 11, 2017, www.investopedia.com/ask/answers/149.asp.

86 Daniel McCarthy and Peter Fader, "Customer-Based Corporate Valuation for
Publicly Traded Non-Contractual Firms," published in the *Journal of Marketing
Research* (2018). Pre-publication version available at SSRN: https://ssrn.com
/abstract=3040422.

87 Alex Morrell, "A New Study Shows Wayfair Is Losing Money on Every New
Customer—and That's Terrible News for the Stock (W)," Business Insider,
September 27, 2017, http://markets.businessinsider.com/news/1002668626.

88 Daniel McCarthy, "Blue Apron's IPO Filing Implies Troubling Customer Retention,"
LinkedIn, June 17, 2017, https://www.linkedin.com/pulse/blue-aprons-ipo-filing
-implies-troubling-customer-daniel-mccarthy.

89 Eliot Brown, "Stir Fry on Sale? Blue Apron Turns to Deals to Draw Customers,"
Wall Street Journal, June 27, 2017, www.wsj.com/articles/stir-fry-on-sale-blue
-apron-turns-to-deals-to-draw-customers-1498561202.

90 Daniel McCarthy, "A Detailed Look at Blue Apron's Challenging Unit Economics,"
LinkedIn, June 27, 2017, www.linkedin.com/pulse/detailed-look-blue-aprons
-challenging-unit-economics-daniel-mccarthy/.

91 For more information, visit https://www.thetaequity.com/.

92 Marshall Fisher, Vishal Gaur, and Herb Kleinberger, "Stop Chasing the Wrong
Kind of Growth," *Harvard Business Review*, January 1, 2017, hbr.org/2017/01
/curing-the-addiction-to-growth. A version of this article appeared in the
January–February 2017 issue (pp. 66–74) of the *Harvard Business Review*.

93 Louis Columbus, "Roundup of Cloud Computing Forecasts, 2017," *Forbes*,
April 29, 2017, www.forbes.com/sites/louiscolumbus/2017/04/29/roundup-of
-cloud-computing-forecasts-2017/#67194f3a31e8.

94 Patrick Campbell, "Data Shows Our Addiction to Acquisition Based Growth Is
Getting Worse," *Price Intelligently* (blog), June 29, 2016, www.priceintelligently
.com/blog/saas-growth-focused-too-much-on-acquisition.

95 G. T. Doran, "There's a S.M.A.R.T. Way to Write Management's Goals and Objectives," *Management Review* 70, no. 11 (1981): 35–36.

96 "Manifesto for Agile Software Development," 2001, agilemanifesto.org/.

97 Barcenas Cruz, "ITIL 101 for Dummies." LinkedIn, July 15, 2015, www.linkedin .com/pulse/itil-101-dummies-francisco-frank-barcenas-cruz.

98 Markey and Reichheld, "Introducing the Net Promoter System."

99 Peter Varhol, "The Complete History of Agile Software Development," TechBeacon, March 28, 2018, techbeacon.com/agility-beyond-history%E2%80%94-legacy%E2% 80%94-agile-development.

100 "Sprint (software development)," TechTarget, June 2015, https://searchsoftware quality.techtarget.com/definition/Scrum-sprint.

101 Forbes Public Relations, "Forbes Announces MLB Team Valuations: Yankees Top the List," Forbes, March 20, 2012, https://www.forbes.com/sites/forbespr /2012/03/20/forbes-announces-mlb-team-valuations-yankees-top-the-list /#74e0098a63d5.

102 Royce Cohen, interview by the author, August 7, 2018.

103 "The Business of Baseball (2018 Ranking)," *Forbes*, 2018, www.forbes.com/mlb -valuations/list/.

104 "Dodgers Accelerator," www.globalsportsventurestudio.com/.

Index

Page numbers in italics refer to figures.

About the Authors

Peter S. Fader is the Frances and Pei-Yuan Chia Professor of Marketing at The Wharton School of the University of Pennsylvania. His expertise centers on topics such as customer relationship management, lifetime value of the customer, and strategies that arise from these data-driven tactics. His work has been published in leading marketing and statistics journals, and he has won many awards for his research and teaching accomplishments. He is the author of *Customer Centricity: Focus on the Right Customers for Strategic Advantage* (2012).

In addition to his activities at Wharton, Professor Fader co-founded a predictive analytics firm (Zodiac) in 2015, which was sold to Nike in 2018. He then co-founded (and continues to run) Theta Equity Partners to commercialize his more recent work on customer-based corporate valuation.

Sarah E. Toms is executive director and cofounder of Wharton Interactive. She is a demonstrated thought leader in the technology field with over two decades experience working in a wide variety of industries. In her positions at Wharton, Sarah has built award-winning *edtech* teams that develop highly engaging games and simulations, which are played by tens of thousands of students globally. Her passion to democratize education led her to co-invent simpl.world, an open-source simulation framework. Sarah was an entrepreneur for more than a decade, founding companies that built global CRM, product development, productivity management, and financial systems. She is a certified ITIL practitioner and led a global ITIL change initiative that touched every aspect of the technology life cycle for a pharmaceutical company.

She is also dedicated to supporting women and girls in technology through her work with the Women in Tech Summit and techgirlz.org.

About Wharton Digital Press

Wharton Digital Press was established to inspire bold, insightful thinking within the global business community. In the tradition of The Wharton School of the University of Pennsylvania and its online business journal, Knowledge@Wharton, Wharton Digital Press uses innovative digital technologies to help managers meet the challenges of today and tomorrow.

As an entrepreneurial publisher, Wharton Digital Press delivers relevant, accessible, conceptually sound, and empirically based business knowledge to readers wherever and whenever they need it. Its format ranges from ebooks to print books available through print-on-demand technology. Directed to a general business audience, the Press's areas of interest include management and strategy, innovation and entrepreneurship, finance and investment, leadership, marketing, operations, human resources, social responsibility, and business–government relations.

http://wdp.wharton.upenn.edu/

About The Wharton School

Founded in 1881 as the first collegiate business school, The Wharton School of the University of Pennsylvania is recognized globally for intellectual leadership and ongoing innovation across every major discipline of business education. With a broad global community and one of the most published business school faculties, Wharton creates economic and social value around the world. The School has 5,000 undergraduate, MBA, executive MBA, and doctoral students; more than 9,200 participants in executive education programs annually; and a powerful alumni network of 98,000 graduates.

http://wharton.upenn.edu/